I0182381

"Wisdom That Transforms. Action That Lasts."

The Get Wisdom Commitment

At Get Wisdom Publishing we believe that true wisdom has the power to transform lives. Our mission is to equip readers with timeless insights and practical tools that inspire growth, guide decisions, and empower purposeful living. We don't just inform—we empower.

Our books combine profound understanding with real-life application, enabling readers to unlock their potential and navigate life's challenges with clarity and confidence. With each step guided by wisdom, we help you create lasting change and live the life you deserve.

When wisdom meets purpose, transformation follows.

Be bold and pray in the Spirit on all occasions.

Copyright

The PRAYER of a Jesus follower: What Scripture Says About Unleashing the Power of God, by Stephen H Berkey, published by Get Wisdom Publishing, Box 465, Thompsons Station, TN 37179, copyright © 2024, Stephen H Berkey

All rights reserved. No portion of this book may be reproduced in any form without written permission from the publisher, except as permitted by U.S. copyright law. For permission contact: info@getwisdompublishing.com

Scriptures marked ESV are taken from THE HOLY BIBLE, ENGLISH STANDARD VERSION®, Copyright© 2001 by Crossway, a publishing ministry of Good News Publishers. Used by permission.

Scriptures marked NLT are taken from the HOLY BIBLE, NEW LIVING TRANSLATION, copyright© 1996, 2004, 2007 by Tyndale House Foundation. Used by permission of Tyndale House Publishers, Inc., Carol Stream, Illinois 60188. All rights reserved. Used by permission.

Scriptures marked HCSB are taken from the HOLMAN CHRISTIAN STANDARD BIBLE (HCSB): Scripture taken from the HOLMAN CHRISTIAN STANDARD BIBLE, copyright© 1999, 2000, 2002, 2003 by Holman Bible Publishers, Nashville Tennessee. All rights reserved.

ISBN   978-1-952359-56-9   (paperback)
ISBN   978-1-952359-57-6   (ebook)

This book is available as an audiobook on our Amazon Jesus Follower Series page:

Unlock Biblical Wisdom and Transform Your Faith

**For more information
about the Jesus Follower Bible Study Series:**
https://getwisdompublishing.com/jesus-follower-series/

Be bold and pray in the Spirit on all occasions.

Jesus Follower Bible Study Series

The PRAYER of a Jesus Follower

What Scripture Says About Unleashing the Power of God!

Stephen H Berkey

GETWISDOM PUBLISHING

This book is available as an audiobook on our Amazon Jesus Follower Series page:

Be bold and pray in the Spirit on all occasions.

Free PDF
Living Wisely

The Life Planning Guide

A Quick-Start Guide to Purposeful Living and Wise Decisions!

Discover the five life domains: purpose, people, principles, productivity, and perspective. Wisdom is the ability to apply truth and logic to real-life decisions and produce good outcomes. It influences your choices and will produce action that lasts. Consider and apply the five practical wisdom principles for daily living. (6 pages)

Free PDF: https://getwisdompublishing.com/resource-registration/

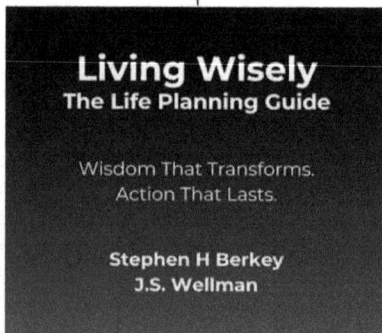

Living Wisely
The Life Planning Guide

Wisdom That Transforms.
Action That Lasts.

Stephen H Berkey
J.S. Wellman

Free PDF

Five Practical Principles For Life

When wisdom meets purpose, transformation follows.

Free PDF
Wise Decision-Making

[Get the ebook version for 99 cents]

You can make good choices.

This free resource provides a project-oriented perspective and gives ten detailed steps to analyze issues/problems to determine a solution. (26 pages)

Good decisions expand your horizons. Don't allow the fear of decision-making paralyze your ability to make good choices. Think through the reasonable alternatives and move forward. When your eyes are on the goal, making good decisions is easier.

Free PDF: https://getwisdompublishing.com/resource-registration/

Kindle ebook for 99 cents: https://www.amazon.com/dp/B09SYGWRVL/

Ebook

Free PDF

Make Thoughtful Decisions!

Good decisions expand your horizons.

Be bold and pray in the Spirit on all occasions.

Effective Life Change
Applying Biblical Wisdom to Live Your Best Life!

Why Read This Book?

- Transform Your life with Biblical Wisdom.
- Cultivate Practical Wisdom in Your life.
- Navigate Life with a Perspective on Biblical Truth.
- Unlock the Proverbs of the Bible to Live Your Best Life.
- Change and Transform Your life.
  Practical Application: These aren't theology or religious discussions, they're practical tools for everyday living.

Get Your Copy Today!

https://www.amazon.com/dp/1952359732
Available in Hardcover, Paperback, Kindle, and Audiobook.

Be bold and pray in the Spirit on all occasions.

The Jesus Follower Journey
Jesus Follower Bible Study Series

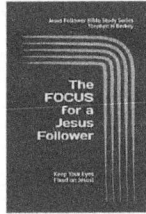

The Jesus Follower Bible Study Series will provide you with a complete description of the nature, characteristics, obligations, commitments, and responsibilities of a true Jesus follower.

Go to our Amazon Book Series page for your copy:
https://www.amazon.com/dp/B0DHP39P5J

The RELATIONSHIP CHARACTERISTICS of a Jesus Follower:
    Are you right with God?
The ONE ANOTHER INSTRUCTIONS to a Jesus Follower:
    Are you right with one another?
The WORSHIP of a Jesus Follower:
    Is your worship acceptable or in vain?
The PRAYER of a Jesus Follower:
    What Scripture says about unleashing the power of God.
The DANGERS of SIN for a Jesus Follower:
    God HATES sin! He abhors sin!
The FOCUS for a Jesus Follower:
    Keep your eyes fixed on Jesus!
The HEART Requirements of a Jesus Follower:
    Follow with all your heart, mind, body, and soul!
The COMMITMENTS of a Jesus Follower:
    Practical Christian living and discipleship.
The OBEDIENCE Requirements for a Jesus Follower:
    Ignore at your own risk!

A related book to this series is, *Effective Life Change: Applying Biblical Wisdom to Live Your Best Life!* This book offers a practical and powerful guide to help navigate life's challenges based on the proverbial wisdom of the Bible. It offers ten commitments that will profoundly change your life.

Table of Contents

Message From the Author

Dear Fellow Christ follower,

Welcome to a journey of faith and discovery.

As the author of this Bible study series, I am excited about the future because I believe this book provides the potential to transform lives, deepen our understanding of God's Word, and ignite a desire within us—a fire that draws us into the presence of our God.

Why read the Jesus Follower Series?

Deeper Roots: We all long for roots that run deep—roots anchored in truth, love, and purpose. In this series, we'll dig into the bedrock of Scripture, unearthing spiritual principles that will guide us in our faith journey.

Authentic Discipleship: Being a Jesus follower isn't about rituals or a superficial commitment. It's about walking the narrow path, picking up your cross, and living a life that loves God, follows Jesus, and loves one another. We will explore what it means to be authentic disciples.

Unveiling Mysteries: God is a source of mysteries and His Word is waiting to be discovered. Together we will examine and encounter the living Word—the One who breathes life into every syllable.

Community and Connection: We are not meant to walk this path alone. As you read, imagine joining a global community of fellow seekers. We will discuss, question, and grow together. Our shared journey will enrich us all. I encourage you to gather friends to join you in this journey.

Expected Benefits:

Renewed Passion: Prepare yourself to wake up each morning with a renewed passion for God's Word. These studies will ignite your hunger for truth and draw you into deeper relationship with the Author of Life.

Practical Application: These aren't theoretical discussions; they're practical tools for everyday living. Expect to see real-life changes—whether it's in your relationships, commitment, or prayer life.

Spiritual Resilience: Life's storms will come, but armed with the insights from God's Word, you can stand firm. Your faith will weather trials, doubts, and uncertainties. You will emerge stronger and more resilient.

Joyful Obedience: As we explore the nature of discipleship, you'll discover that obedience isn't a burden—it's a joy. The path of obedience leads to peace, and you'll find yourself saying, "Yes, Lord!" with newfound delight.

Let's Begin!

So, turn the page. Dive into the first chapter. Let the words seep into your soul. And remember, you're not alone—we're on this pilgrimage together. May these books be more than ink on paper; may they be stepping stones toward a life that leads to eternity. Amen!

"We believe applied wisdom empowers life change. Our books provide clarity, inspiration, and tools to equip readers to live their best life."

My prayer is that you will

Be tenacious like Job
Walk like Enoch
Believe like Abraham
Wrestle like Jacob
Dress like Joseph
Lead like Moses
Conquer like Deborah
Be fearless like Shamgar
Inspire like Josuha
Influence like Esther
Dance like David
Ask like Jabez
Have the faith of Daniel
Pray like Elijah
Trust like Elisha
Commit like Isaiah
Be courageous like Benaiah
Rebuild like Nehemiah
Be obedient like Hosea
Be zealous like Zacchaeus
Surrender like Mary
Stand firm like Stephen
Speak like Peter
Seize opportunities like Philip
Submit like Paul
Overcome like the Elect (Saints)
Worship like the 24 Elders
and
Love like Jesus

Steve

Introduction

BOOK DESCRIPTION – Unlock the Power of Prayer

Unlock the power of prayer in your life with "The PRAYER of a Jesus Follower." Are you yearning for a deeper connection with God and wondering why your prayers sometimes feel unanswered? This transformative Bible study dives into the heart of prayer, exploring what Scripture truly reveals about this vital conversation with our Creator. You can change your prayer life forever, but you must align your desires with His will. What barriers might be standing in the way of your prayers being answered?

This study is inspired by 1 John 5:14-15, which assures us that God hears and answers prayers aligned with His will. The lessons go beyond theory to reveal the practical steps that connect our hearts with His divine purpose. Each lesson equips you with essential knowledge from Scripture. You will understand the conditions necessary for answered prayer in order to overcome hindrances that may impede your spiritual journey.

In this insightful study, you will explore:

- **The Conditions for Answered Prayer:** Understand the essential steps you can take to ensure your prayers resonate with God's heart.
- **Effective Prayer Practices:** Learn how to pray with intention and purpose, experiencing the transformative power of effective communication with God.

- **Overcoming Hindrances:** Gain clarity on what might be blocking your prayers and learn how to overcome these obstacles.
- **The Power of Fasting:** Discover the profound connection between fasting and prayer, and how this practice can elevate your spiritual journey.
- **Praying with Boldness:** Embrace the courage to "ask big" as demonstrated in the Prayer of Jabez. Explore the significance of praying boldly. Watch as your faith flourishes.

Comprehensive and Practical. With engaging lessons, practical applications, and rich biblical insights, "The PRAYER of a Jesus Follower" is an invitation to experience the fullness of life that comes from a vibrant prayer life. You'll find appendices filled with Jesus' and Paul's prayers, the Lord's Prayer, and essential facts that will enhance your understanding and prayer life.

Transform Your Prayer Life Today. This book will equip you with the knowledge and confidence to pray boldly, expect answers, and witness the incredible impact of a committed prayer life. Don't just read about prayer— experience it!

REASONS TO PRAY

Why is prayer important? Why should we pray? Consider these seven reasons from Scripture:

- Prayer is essential to our relationship with Christ. John 15:7
- Prayer is the key to heaven's resources. James 4:2
- Prayer delights God. Proverbs 15:8
- Prayer is the key to our peace of mind. Philippians 4:6-7
- Prayer is the key to our effectiveness. John 15:5
- Prayer brings God's spiritual power. James 5:16

- Prayer is the source of joy.   John 16:24
- Prayer is desired by Jesus.   Luke 18:1

E. M. Bounds says that "activity without prayer is pride and prayer without activity is presumption." Think about what Bounds is saying here. We must ask for God's help, but we must also do our share. Bounds defines the goal of prayer as "attaining the ear of God." He says, "This goal can be reached only by patient and continued waiting on our Lord, pouring out our hearts to him and permitting him to speak to us. Only by so doing can we expect to know him, and as we come to know him better we shall spend more time in his presence and find his presence a constant and ever increasing delight."[1]

IMPORTANT BIBLICAL PROMISES

HE HEARS: *The Lord is far from the wicked, but he hears the prayers of the righteous.* (Pr 15:29 NLT)

HE ANSWERS: [God says,] *I will answer them before they even call to me. While they are still talking about their needs, I will go ahead and answer their prayers!* (Isa 65:24 NLT)

HE RESPONDS: *O people of Zion, who live in Jerusalem, you will weep no more. He will be gracious if you ask for help. He will surely respond to the sound of your cries.* (Isa 30:19 NLT)

HE INFORMS: *Ask me and I will tell you remarkable secrets you do not know about things to come.* (Jer 33:3-4 NLT)

HE GIVES WISDOM: *If you need wisdom, ask our generous God, and he will give it to you. He will not rebuke you for asking.* (James 1:5-6 NLT)

HE HELPS: *And the Holy Spirit helps us in our weakness. For example, we don't know what God wants us to pray for. But the Holy Spirit prays for us with groanings that cannot be expressed in words.* (Romans 8:26-27 NLT)

HE RESCUES: *When they call on me, I will answer; I will be with them in trouble. I will rescue and honor them.* (Ps 91:15 NLT)

HE PROVIDES MERCY AND GRACE: *So let us come boldly to the throne of our gracious God. There we will receive his mercy, and we will find grace to help us when we need it most.* (Hebrews 4:16 NLT)

HE HEALS: *Confess your sins to each other and pray for each other so that you may be healed. The earnest prayer of a righteous person has great power and produces wonderful results.* (James 5:16-17 NLT)

HE GIVES WISDOM: *Call to me and I will answer you and tell you great and unsearchable things you do not know.* (Jer 33:3 NLT)

HE BRINGS PEACE: *Do not be anxious about anything, but in everything, by prayer and petition, with thanksgiving, present your requests to God. And the peace of God, which transcends all understanding, will guard your hearts and your minds in Christ Jesus.* (Phil 4:6-7 NLT)

HE PROTECTS: *Watch and pray so that you will not fall into temptation . . .* (Matt 26:41 NLT)

HE IS WITH US: *. . . if two of you on earth agree about anything you ask for, it will be done for you by my Father in heaven. For where two or three come together in my name, there am I with them."* (Matt 18:19-20 NLT)

WHAT ARE YOU EXPECTING?

Prayer can be frustrating if we have the wrong perspective and misguided expectations about what God is going to do. We can be confused if He doesn't answer our requests in a timely manner. God will generally provide what we need rather than what we ask for. An easy illustration is praying for a new car, maybe specifically a full size SUV. What God provides is transportation which may be in the form of a used car, a neighbor who acts as our driver when needed, or money for public transportation. We should think about real <u>needs</u> before we pray.

If our expectations are for an expensive impressive luxury vehicle, we may think God did not answer our prayer for transportation when we end up with a used Chevy. If we pray for patience do we expect God to give us patience, or is He more likely to give us opportunities to be patient? If we pray for courage, is God going to give us courage, or will He give us opportunities to be courageous? If we ask God to bring our family closer together, do we expect God to zap the family and give us all warm fuzzy feelings for each other? Or is He more likely going to give us opportunities to love each other?[2]

Group Discussion or Individual Study

These studies can be done individually or in a small discussion group. An important value of the study is in the discussion questions. We all see life differently and the thoughts and ideas shared in a group will often lead to a richer understanding of the Scripture. We recommend doing these studies in a group, if possible.

Format of Lessons

The format of the lessons is not the same in each book. We chose a format that best fit the material.

LESSON 1

What Conditions are Necessary for Answered Prayer?

"I think Christians fail so often to get
answers to their prayers because they
do not wait long enough on God."
E. M. Bounds[3]

It's easy to say that God answers prayer with either a "yes, no, or wait." If we want answers, it is first necessary to get the ear of God. God's Word puts certain conditions on His response. For prayer to be effective, we must understand the biblical requirements.

The Primary Condition #1

Question 1: What are the two similar but different conditions for answered prayer in the following?

Mark 11:22-24 *And Jesus answered them, "Have faith in God. 23 Truly, I say to you, whoever says to this mountain, 'Be taken up and thrown into the sea,' and does not doubt in his heart, but believes that what he says will come to pass, it will be done for him. 24 Therefore I tell you, whatever you ask in prayer, believe that you have received it, and it will be yours.* ESV [Also Mt 21:21-22]

(a)

(b)

Note the following verses that support each of the conditions stated above. Underline the key phrases in these passages.

James 1:6-8 *But let him ask in faith, with no doubting, for the one who doubts is like a wave of the sea that is driven and tossed by the wind. 7 For that person must not suppose that he will receive anything from the Lord; 8 he is a double-minded man, unstable in all his ways.* ESV

Hebrews 11:6 *And without faith it is impossible to please him, for whoever would draw near to God must believe that he exists and that he rewards those who seek him.* ESV

Question 2: Is it faith in Christ or is it faith/belief that God will answer? Why?

Question 3: What does Romans 4:20-21 confirm?
Romans 4:20-21 *No distrust made him waver concerning the promise of God, but he grew strong in his faith as he gave glory to God, 21 fully convinced that God was able to do what he had promised.* ESV

Question 4: Based on Romans 10:17, what is the source of our faith?
Romans 10:17 *So faith comes from hearing, and hearing through the word of Christ.* ESV

Question 5: When you pray do you really believe God is going to answer, or are you just hoping?

The first time I taught this class using these notes, one of the participants put his finger on what many of us were thinking: "I *know* God will answer, and I *hope* he will answer the way I want." I am sure many of us feel that way at times. But what if you are just "hoping" and not believing? If you have doubts, what are your doubts? Are you lacking in faith, or are you just not totally persuaded? Are you concerned you are praying outside the will of God?

Condition #2

1 John 5:14-15 *And this is the confidence that we have toward him, that if we ask anything according to his will he hears us. 15 And if we know that he hears us in whatever we ask, we know that we have the requests that we have asked of him.* ESV

Question 6: What does "according to His will" (in the above verse) mean <u>to you personally</u>? (Discuss)

Question 7: What does "according to His will" mean or imply biblically?

Question 8: Review the following verses and record your thoughts and observations under each Scripture.

John 6:38-39 *For I have come down from heaven, not to do my own will but the will of him who sent me. 39 And this is the will of him who sent me, that I should lose nothing of all that he has given me, but raise it up on the last day.* ESV

Romans 12:2 *Do not be conformed to this world, but be transformed by the renewal of your mind, that by testing you may discern what is the will of God, what is good and acceptable and perfe*ct. ESV

Ephesians 1:11 *In him we have obtained an inheritance, having been predestined according to the purpose of him who works all things according to the counsel of his will,* ESV

1 Thessalonians 4:3 *For this is the will of God, your sanctification: that you abstain from sexual immorality;* ESV [To understand the context and focus of this reference to sanctification, read verses 4-8 that follow this verse].

Perhaps all this could be summed up by the following verse from Jeremiah:

Jeremiah 29:12-13 *Then you will call upon me and come and pray to me, and I will hear you. 13 You will seek me and find me. When you seek me with all your heart* ESV

Jeremiah says we are to seek Him *with all our heart.*

Question 9: How might you summarize Jeremiah 29:12-13?

Condition #3

God's Word requires obedience. It should not be surprising that obeying God's commands would be a condition for answered prayer. How can we expect God to do what we ask unless we do what He asks? Our disobedience began with Adam and we are burdened with a sinful nature. We must fight and resist that nature at every turn; it is natural for us to desire what the carnal world has to offer.

Question 10: What are the two conditions outlined in the following Scripture?

> **1 John 3:22-23** . . . *and whatever we ask we receive from him, because we keep his commandments and do what pleases him. 23 And this is his commandment, that we believe in the name of his Son Jesus Christ and love one another, just as he has commanded us.* ESV

(a)

(b)

Question 11: What does it say this command means?

(a)

(b)

Question 12: What do Hebrews 11:6 and Proverbs 15:8 say pleases Him?

Prov 15:8

Heb 11:6

Question 13: What does "upright" in Proverbs 15:8 mean?

Condition #4

Question 14: What is the condition outlined in these two verses from John?

John 14:13 *Whatever you ask in my name, this I will do, that the Father may be glorified in the Son.* ESV

John 16:24 *Until now you have asked nothing in my name. Ask, and you will receive, that your joy may be full.* ESV

Question 15: Does the above mean we need to remember to invoke the name of Jesus when we pray, or does it mean more? In the ancient world what was associated with a "name?"

Question 16: What does Philippians 2:9-11 say about Jesus' name?

Philippians 2:9-11 *Therefore God has highly exalted him and bestowed on him the name that is above every name, 10 so that at the name of Jesus every knee should bow, in heaven and on earth and under the earth, 11 and every tongue confess that Jesus Christ is Lord, to the glory of God the Father.* ESV

Condition #5

Question 17: What are the two conditions outlined in John 15:7?

John 15:7 *If you abide in me, and my words abide in you, ask whatever you wish, and it will be done for you.* ESV

(a)

(b)

Note the consistency with Paul's instructions in the following two passages:

Ephesians 6:18 . . . *praying at all times __in the Spirit__, with all prayer and supplication. To that end keep alert with all perseverance, making supplication for all the saints.* ESV
Jude 20 *But you, beloved, build yourselves up in your most holy faith; __pray in the Holy Spirit__.* ESV

Abiding (or "remaining") in Jesus implies:

- fervency in prayer and worship
- dependence due to surrender and submission
- intense level of communion with Him

- loving obedience
- close, constant, intimate relationship

Abiding doesn't describe how much you know about your faith, who you know, what you do, or what office you hold. It is describing the nature of your relationship with Christ! Abiding might be described by the following terms:

seek after	long for	thirst after
wait for	trust in	know
love	spend time with	commit to
hope in	be still before	rely on
delight in	take refuge in	

We think the best phrase above that describes abiding is "rely on." I wait upon the Lord, I follow His lead, and thus I *rely on* Him. Abiding is a form of surrender to Christ — I put myself in His hands and I allow Him to direct my life.

Abiding is NOT an end in itself. The result of abiding is that we demonstrate love, walk in obedience, stand firm, and bear fruit. The sap of life flows through the branches from the Vine. It is the life-giving power from the Divine that produces the fruit.

Remember that the Bible specifically tells us that God can overcome all the hurdles we have in front of us. We can be overcomers, because 1 John 4:4 says that God who indwells His followers is greater than anyone in the world.

Paul described one of the functions of the indwelling Holy Spirit as follows:

Romans 8:26-27 *Likewise the Spirit helps us in our weakness. For we do not know what to pray for as we ought, but the Spirit himself intercedes for us with groanings too deep for words. 27 And he who searches* *hearts knows what is the mind of the Spirit, because the Spirit intercedes for the saints according to the will of God.* ESV

The Holy Spirit is interceding for us!

Question 18: What do the two conditions about abiding in John 15:7 mean to you? Do you think they mean the same thing?

Condition #6

Question 19: What condition is identified in John 15:8, 16?
John 15:8 *By this my Father is glorified, that you bear much fruit and so prove to be my disciples.* ESV
John 15:16 *You did not choose me, but I chose you and appointed you that you should go and bear fruit and that your fruit should abide, so that whatever you ask the Father in my name, he may give it to you.* ESV

Question 20: Based on each of the following verses, what is to be our focus in bearing fruit?
Ephesians 4:12 *. . . to equip the saints for the work of ministry, for building up the body of Christ,* ESV
Romans 12:7 *. . . if service, in our serving; the one who teaches, in his teaching;* ESV
1 Peter 4:10 *As each has received a gift, use it to serve one another, as good stewards of God's varied grace* ESV

Ephesians 4:12

Romans 12:7

1 Peter 4:10

Question 21: What is the significance in John 15:16 of "fruit that will last?"

SUMMARY

Question 22: Summarize the six to eight conditions identified above by listing them here:

1. (a)_____
   (b)_____
2. _____
3. _____
4. _____
5. (a)_____
   (b)_____
6. _____

All these verses include a promise to answer prayer if the given conditions are met. If you review those verses you will observe that in every case they have some phrase like "receive what you ask." Underline or highlight the promise to answer in each key verse.

CONCLUSION

We can conclude from the above that the practice of prayer is more than just praying for ourselves and others.

It is a lifestyle and attitude of yielding our lives to the will of God. Can you think of any type of relationship that can survive without communication? E. M. Bounds in *Purpose in Prayer*, says, "Prayer and a holy life are one. . . Neither can survive alone. The absence of one is the absence of the other. . . We are in danger of substituting churchly work and a ceaseless round of showy activities for prayer and holy living."

God's Word tells us how to be effective in prayer, what to avoid, why to pray, and what to pray for. We'll look at these issues in the next few lessons.

DISCUSSION AND THOUGHT QUESTIONS

1. Can any of these conditions be isolated and claimed apart from the others? Why or why not?

2. Do these conditions seem overwhelming or burdensome?

3. If you were to describe all of these conditions in total to someone else, how would you characterize them?

4. Why do you think God establishes these conditions?

5. Given these conditions, will God answer the prayer of unbelievers?

6. With the exception of Condition #2, what is a common thread that runs through all the conditions?

What I Want to Remember

Enter some notes and information that you want to remember about this lesson. It might be a Scripture verse or two, something new you learned, something you want to do, something you want to change, or just something you want to be sure to remember.

Wisdom to Action
Challenge

In what areas of your life do you need to better align with God's will? How can you actively seek to abide in Christ more fully through your daily choices and actions?

LESSON 2
How Can I Be Effective in Prayer?

Search me, O God, and know my heart;
test me and know my anxious thoughts.
See if there is any offensive way in me,
and lead me in the way everlasting.
Psalm 139:23-24

Although the characteristics given in the following verses are extremely important for effective prayer, they do not have the same degree of "requirement" as the conditions outlined in Lesson 1. All of the verses in the previous lesson included a promise to answer prayer. The following verses do not have that same promise (with the possible exceptions of Psalm 37:4 and Matthew 7:8).

Review the following verses and note the characteristics that will make your prayer effective.

GENERAL CHARACTERISTICS GOD IS SEEKING

The following two passages could almost be conditional statements to answered prayer similar to those in Lesson 1, except they do not specifically promise an answer:

Proverbs 15:8 *The sacrifice of the wicked is an abomination to the Lord, but the prayer of the upright is acceptable to him.* ESV

James 5:16 *Therefore, confess your sins to one another and pray for one another, that you may be healed. The*

prayer of a <u>righteous</u> person has great power as it is working. ESV

Q1: What does it mean to be upright and righteous?

upright:

righteous:

WHAT COMMITMENT DOES GOD WANT?

Colossians 4:2 *Continue <u>steadfastly</u> in prayer, being <u>watchful</u> in it <u>with thanksgiving</u>.* ESV

Q2: What do you think Col 4:2 means?

Q3: What does Colossians 3:23, imply about prayer?
Colossians 3:23 *Whatever you do, work heartily, as for the Lord and not for men.* ESV

A theme running throughout these "instructions" is commitment. You must be committed to both your faith and Christ as well as to the task of prayer. It seems obvious that half-hearted attempts at calling on the power of God are not likely to get His attention. Think about this like the difference between whispering and shouting. If you are not invested enough to make sure God hears you, you may not really believe what you are whispering about. God apparently wants us to give ourselves fully to this task.

Note the words "ask," "seek," and "knock" in the following passage. The Greek form used for these words means a continuing process. Thus, our prayer must be continuing or ongoing. It is not to be one-off praying.

Matt 7:7-11 *"Ask, and it will be given to you; seek, and you will find; knock, and it will be opened to you. 8 For everyone who asks receives, and the one who seeks finds, and to the one who knocks it will be opened. 9 Or which one of you, if his son asks him for bread, will give him a stone? 10 Or if he asks for a fish, will give him a serpent? 11 If you then, who are evil, know how to give good gifts to your children, how much more will your Father who is in heaven give good things to those who ask him!* ESV

Q4: What do you think it means to "be committed" to something and how might this apply to prayer?

E. M. Bounds has said, "Too often we get faint-hearted and quit praying at the point where we ought to begin. We let go at the very point where we should hold on the strongest. Our prayers are weak because they are not impassioned by an unfailing and irresistible will."[4]

It is instructive to remember the parable of Luke 18:2-8 about the widow who kept hounding a judge to provide what she needed. You may wonder when you can stop praying? The answer is likely, "When something happens!"

Q5: What was the parable described in Luke 18:2-8 intended to teach? How do you know?

There is little doubt that a great deal of our failure in prayer is our inability to persevere. We lack persistency! Persistency is the hallmark of good praying. Jesus clearly wants us to understand that we should not give up. We fail because we quit too soon. It may be that we give up at just the time our praying is needed most. Our motto should be to P.U.S.H.

Pray Until Something Happens.

Is patience a big stumbling block for you? If it is, give it over to Him and wait patiently!

WHILE WAITING: PRAISE GOD!

Psalms 37:4 *Delight yourself in the Lord, and he will give you the desires of your heart.* ESV

The Greek base word for "delight" in this verse is "hallal" or ***praise***. David praised God in the Psalms. Praising God is the expression of approval, gratitude, or admiration for His character or works (acts). Psalms 145-150 are great psalms of praise — take some time to read all or parts of these five Psalms. Praise in our prayers can be a powerful force. Look up and record what important characteristics of praise are described in the following. We have done the first and last ones.

Psalm 29:2   Praise honors God the Father

Psalm 22:3

2 Chronicles 5:13

Acts 16:25-26

Psalm 150:2

Psalm 119:164   Do it regularly

Note in 2 Chronicles 20:12, Psalm 8:2, and Psalm 149:5-9 that praise even confuses the forces of evil or darkness. It almost seems mandatory that our prayers include praise! We should acknowledge who God is, what He has done, what He can do, and give Him praise and thanksgiving.

Remember praise is an expression of gratitude or thanksgiving for God's character or His works. Praise occurs as the result of his mercy and grace, because we certainly don't deserve His love or His forgiveness — or at least I don't. Psalm 150:2 says we are to praise Him for his deeds and greatness, while Psalm 119:164 suggests we praise Him for keeping everything working right (His rules, ordinances, regulations).

WAITING ON THE LORD

Psalms 27:14 *Wait for the Lord; be strong, and let your heart take courage; wait for the Lord!* ESV

Psalms 37:7 *Be still before the Lord and wait patiently for him; fret not yourself over the one who prospers in his way, over the man who carries out evil devices!* ESV

Psalms 37:9 *For the evildoers shall be cut off, but those who wait for the Lord shall inherit the land.* ESV

Psalms 37:34 *Wait for the Lord and keep his way, and he will exalt you to inherit the land; you will look on when the wicked are cut off.* ESV

Psalms 40:1 *I waited patiently for the Lord; he inclined to me and heard my cry.* ESV

Until recently I assumed these passages about waiting were referring to being patient, but then I read the

Hebrew meaning of the word. It means far more than just waiting! The Hebrew meaning includes the concept of being intertwined or twisted together. Like a rope, the strands are twisted together to make the rope stronger because they are melded into one.

That really changes the understanding of what it means to "Wait upon the LORD!"

Q6: How would you now answer the question of what it means to "Give yourself fully to the work of the Lord?" What words or phrases would you choose to describe "waiting?"

HUMBLE YOURSELVES BEFORE THE LORD!

James 4:10 *Humble yourselves before the Lord, and he will exalt you.* ESV

2 Chronicles 7:14 *if my people who are called by my name humble themselves, and pray and seek my face and turn from their wicked ways, then I will hear from heaven and will forgive their sin and heal their land.* ESV

Q7: What do you think it means to "humble yourself?"

Let's allow Scripture to determine what this means. Look at the following Scriptures to determine what they say about being humble.

2 Kings 22:19 . . . *because your heart was penitent, and you humbled yourself before the Lord, when you heard how I spoke against this place and against its inhabitants, that they should become a desolation and a curse, and you have torn your clothes and wept before me, I also have heard you, declares the Lord.* ESV

Proverbs 3:34 *Toward the scorners he is scornful, but to the humble he gives favor.* ESV

Luke 18:13-14 *But the tax collector, standing far off, would not even lift up his eyes to heaven, but beat his breast, saying, 'God, be merciful to me, a sinner!' 14 I tell you, this man went down to his house justified, rather than the other.* For everyone who exalts himself will be humbled, but the one who humbles himself will be exalted." ESV

Psalm 35:13 *But I, when they were sick—I wore sackcloth; I afflicted myself with fasting; I prayed with head bowed on my chest.* ESV

Q8: Look up the following Scriptures and record what they say will be the result of being humble before the Lord?

James 4:10

2 Chronicles 7:14

2 Kings 22:20

Proverbs 3:34

Luke 18:13-14

LISTEN – IT'S NOT ALL TALK

Psalms 85:8 *Let me hear what God the Lord will speak, for he will speak peace to his people, to his saints; but let them not turn back to folly.* ESV

Isa 55:2-3 *Why do you spend your money for that which is not bread, and your labor for that which does not satisfy? Listen diligently to me, and eat what is good, and delight yourselves in rich food. 3 Incline your ear, and come to me; hear, that your soul may live; and I will make with you an everlasting covenant, my steadfast, sure love for David.* ESV

Q9: What are we to do based on the above passages?

Listening and really hearing what is being said can sometimes be very difficult, particularly if we are distracted or not giving our full attention. How do we best do this?

Q10. What would make us more effective at listening?

Q11. What advice do we receive from Ecclesiastes 5:1-2?
Ecclesiastes 5:1-2 Fear God
Guard your steps when you go to the house of God. To draw near to listen is better than to offer the sacrifice of fools, for they do not know that they are doing evil. 2 Be not rash with your mouth, nor let your heart be hasty to utter a word before God, for God is in heaven and you are on earth. Therefore let your words be few. ESV

AN IMPORTANT ATTITUDE: CONFIDENCE

Ephesians 3:12 . . . *in whom we have boldness and access with <u>confidence</u> through our faith in him. ESV*
Hebrews 4:16 *Let us then with <u>confidence</u> draw near to the throne of grace, that we may receive mercy and find grace to help in time of need. ESV*

Q12: According to the above and Ro 4:21, what should be the basis of this confidence?
Romans 4:21 . . . *fully convinced that God was able to do what he had promised. ESV*

BIBLICAL PRAYER SUCCESS

The result of answered prayer in the Bible made a significant impact on a broad spectrum of things, people, and events. For example:

1. Jabez prayed for enlarged borders and protection from harm (1 Chronicles 4:10 see Lesson 7)
2. Other people in the Bible prayed for deliverance from trouble (Psalm 34:15-22)
3. Deliverance from both poverty and riches (Prov 30:7-9)
4. Deliverance from the belly of a great fish (Jonah 2:7-10)
5. Daily bread (Matt. 6:11)
6. Preservation and sanctification of spirit, soul, and body (1 Thessalonians 5:23)
7. The healing of the sick (James 5:14-15)
8. The end of the rain and its beginning again (James 5:17-18)

See additional examples in Appendix E

Question 13: What can we pray and know we will always be praying the will of God based on Colossians 1:9-12?
Colossians 1:9-12 *And so, from the day we heard, we have not ceased to pray for you, asking that you may be filled with the knowledge of his will in all spiritual wisdom and understanding, 10 so as to walk in a manner worthy of the Lord, fully pleasing to him, bearing fruit in every good work and increasing in the knowledge of God. 11 May you be strengthened with all power, according to his glorious might, for all endurance and patience with joy, 12 giving thanks to the Father, who has qualified you to share in the inheritance of the saints in light.* ESV

Question 14: Can you list ten actions from this lesson that would identify how to be effective in prayer?

1.

2.

3.

4.

5.

6.

7.

8.

9.

10.

What I Want to Remember

Enter some notes and information that you want to remember about this lesson. It might be a Scripture verse or two, something new you learned, something you want to do, something you want to change, or just something you want to be sure to remember.

Wisdom to Action
Challenge

What sins or unresolved conflicts might be hindering your prayers? How will you address these issues to maintain an open channel of communication with God?

LESSON 3
What are the Hindrances to Answered Prayer?

It was I who knew you in the wilderness,
in the land of drought; but when they
had grazed, they became full, they were filled,
and their heart was lifted up;
therefore they forgot me.
Hosea 13:5-6 NLT

In Lesson 1 we studied the conditions necessary for us to expect answers to prayer and in Lesson 2 we reviewed what activities make prayer more effective. If we choose not to follow the guidelines outlined in these lessons, it will negatively impact God's desire to answer prayer. The Bible speaks of certain other specific issues that hinder prayer. In this lesson we will take a closer look at what the Bible specifically says will obstruct our ability to receive answers to prayer.

THE GENERAL PROBLEM

Common sense tells us that things like sin and rebellion against God will stand in the way of getting prayers answered. Both the Old and New Testaments confirm that thinking:

> **Psalms 66:17-18** *I cried to him with my mouth, and high praise was on my tongue. 18 If I had cherished iniquity in my heart, the Lord would not have listened.* ESV

1 Peter 3:12 *For the eyes of the Lord are on the righteous, and his ears are open to their prayer. But the face of the Lord is <u>against those who do evil</u>.* ESV

We know from John 9:31 that God does not listen to the prayers of sinful people. Scripture says specifically that God listens to righteous people who do His will (obedient). This was confirmed in Lesson 1, Condition #2, where we learned it is necessary to pray according to His will.

In reading Matthew 5:21-30 we gain the understanding that sin is more than just doing something wrong: it is also an attitude. Psalm 51:4 makes it clear that sin is rebellion against the laws of God. If you're not too sure about this, review Genesis 39:9, 2 Samuel 12:13, and Luke 15:18.

We must be careful not to take John 9:31 about God not listening out of context. It does not necessarily pertain to unbelievers. Since we are all sinners this verse likely pertains to those who deliberately sin, live in sin, and do not repent of their sin.

Question 1a: God will deal with the reality of sin. What do the following verses tell us about sin?

2 Samuel 24:1 *Again the anger of the Lord was kindled against Israel, and he incited David against them, saying, "Go, number Israel and Judah."* ESV

1 Chronicles 21:1 *Then Satan stood against Israel and incited David to number Israel.* ESV

Acts 17:28 *In him we live and move and have our being; as even some of your own poets have said, "For we are indeed his offspring."* ESV

1 John 1:10 *If we say we have not sinned, we make him a liar, and his word is not in us.* ESV

THE GOOD NEWS ABOUT SIN

Mark 2:17 *And when Jesus heard it, he said to them, "Those who are well have no need of a physician, but those who are sick. I came not to call the righteous, but sinners."* ESV

1 John 1:7, 9 *But if we walk in the light, as he is in the light, we have fellowship with one another, and the blood of Jesus his Son cleanses us from all sin. . . . If we confess our sins, he is faithful and just to forgive us our sins and to cleanse us from all unrighteousness.* ESV

The absolute saving grace for the sinner is the fact that even though we sin, He will forgive and cleanse us from all unrighteousness! But this assumes we are a believer: *"Whoever confesses that Jesus is the Son of God, God abides in him, and he in God."* (1 John 4:15 ESV)

Remember that John 15:7 says, *"If you abide in me, and my words abide in you, ask whatever you wish, and it will be done for you."* (ESV) We can conclude from all of the above that in order to assure that God is listening and likely to respond positively:

- our prayer must come from our heart,

- we must have true belief, and

- we must know and live now Christ's teachings.

WHAT SPECIFIC SINS HINDER OUR PRAYER LIFE?

Question 1b. Each of the following verses identifies a specific sin that can hinder our prayer life, what is it?

Isaiah 29:13 *And the Lord said: "Because this people draw near with their mouth and honor me with their lips, while their hearts are far from me, and their fear of me is a commandment taught by men.* ESV

Malachi 1:7-8 *By offering polluted food upon my altar. But you say, 'How have we polluted you?' By saying that the Lord's table may be despised. 8 When you offer blind animals in sacrifice, is that not evil? And when you offer those that are lame or sick, is that not evil? Present that to your governor; will he accept you or show you favor? says the Lord of hosts.* ESV

Matthew 15:9 *. . . in vain do they worship me, teaching as doctrines the commandments of men.* ESV

Question 2: What is the common thread in the above verses? What are some examples of rules or "commandments taught by men"?

Thread:

Rules:

CHEATING GOD

Malachi describes above that the people were bringing defiled food to the altar, and he described this as being "evil." The people were cheating on God by giving Him the blind, lame, or sick animals and keeping the good ones for themselves.

Question 3: How do we pollute, cheat or rob God today?

HYPOCRITES

Matthew 6:5-7 *And when you pray, you must not be like the hypocrites. For they love to stand and pray in the synagogues and at the street corners, that they may be seen by others. . . . 6 But when you pray, go into your room and shut the door and pray to your Father who is in secret. And your Father who sees in secret will reward you. 7 And when you pray, do not heap up empty phrases as the Gentiles do, for they think that they will be heard for their many words.* ESV

Luke 18:11-14 *The Pharisee, standing by himself, prayed thus: God, I thank you that I am not like other men, extortioners, unjust, adulterers, or even like this tax collector. 12 I fast twice a week; I give tithes of all that I get. 13 But the tax collector, standing far off, would not even lift up his eyes to heaven, but beat his breast, saying,*

God, be merciful to me, a sinner! 14 I tell you, this man went down to his house justified, rather than the other. For everyone who exalts himself will be humbled, but the one who humbles himself will be exalted. ESV

Question 4: What is the specific sin being described above?

Question 5: How do people today generally act like hypocrites in the church?

Question 6: How has pride impacted you personally, your relationship with Jesus, or your prayer life today?

ARE SPECIFIC REQUESTS IMPORTANT

James 4:3 *You ask and do not receive, because you ask wrongly, to spend it on your passions.* ESV

Question 7: What are some examples of "asking wrongly"?

Question 8: What are examples of prayers that would be for our own pleasures or passions?

We can identify at least five motives for prayer that are consistent with the instruction in James 4:3 to not "ask wrongly" or to "ask with the wrong motives." God wants us to pray such that it will:

- fit His will,
- benefit His kingdom,
- benefit others,
- provide forgiveness, or
- be consistent with his Word.

Question 9: What is the sin in the following proverb?
Proverbs 28:9 *If one turns away his ear from hearing the law, even his prayer is an abomination.* ESV

Question 10: What does Matthew 5:16 tell us should be the result of our prayer/deeds?
Matthew 5:16 *In the same way, let your light shine before others, so that they may see your good works and give glory to your Father who is in heaven.* ESV

RELATIONSHIPS

In the following verse from Mark 11:25 the issue is the sin of unresolved conflict or relationships: "*And whenever you stand praying, forgive, if you have anything against anyone, so that your Father also who is in heaven may forgive you your trespasses.*" ESV This could also refer to the lack of forgiveness.

Peter also discusses the negative impact on prayer in the family:

1 Peter 3:7 *Likewise, husbands, live with your wives in an understanding way, showing honor to the woman as the weaker vessel, since they are heirs with you of the grace of life, so that your prayers may not be hindered.* ESV

Question 11: Why would God single out the wife (spouse) for this type of importance in regard to prayer?
[Can you find a passage in Scripture that would support your answer?]

DIFFICULTY PRAYING? NO WORRIES!

When some people experience difficulty praying, they find it helpful simply to listen. We'll talk about listening later in this study, but consider if your difficulty could be overcome by better listening. Are you monopolizing the conversation? God tells us over and over that He will help during times of difficulty. Review the following verses and note who is helping in our prayers:

Hebrews 7:25 *Consequently, he [**Jesus**] is able to save to the uttermost those who draw near to God through him, since he always lives to make intercession for them.* ESV

Romans 8:34 *Who is to condemn? **Christ Jesus** is the one who died, more than that, who was raised, who is at the right hand of God, who indeed is interceding for us.* ESV

Romans 8:26-27 *Likewise the Spirit helps us in our weakness. For we do not know what to pray for as we ought, but the **Spirit himself** intercedes for us with groanings too deep for words. 27 And he who searches hearts knows what is the mind of the Spirit, because the Spirit intercedes for the saints according to the will of God.* ESV

47

The Godhead is able to save completely those who come to Him. Jesus and the Holy Spirit are all interceding on our behalf. And God says:

- before we pray He will answer (Isaiah 65:24)
- He knows what we need even before we ask (Matthew 6:8)

Even when we're not sure what to pray, God knows our need and He knows the answer. In this life we may never understand His plan, His sovereignty, His wishes or his wisdom, but we can pray that His will be done and seek His presence in our life *"with all our heart."* And we should recognize that the best news is that prayer is so important to God that the entire Godhead (Father, Son and Holy Spirit) are all engaged in helping us in prayer.

DISCUSSION OR THOUGHT QUESTIONS

Question 12: Can you relate any personal experience when you have had difficulty praying and how you overcame that difficulty?

Question 13: What are the biggest obstacles you personally encounter in finding time to pray?

Question 14: What characteristics of effective prayer need work in your prayer life?

Question 15: Do you have a roadblock in your prayer life? How could you overcome it?

Question 16: What does it take to displace or cancel your prayer time?

Question 17: Is prayer a priority in your life today? Why? Why not?

What I Want to Remember

Enter some notes and information that you want to remember about this lesson. It might be a Scripture verse or two, something new you learned, something you want to do, something you want to change, or just something you want to be sure to remember.

Wisdom to Action
Challenge

What practical steps can you take to cultivate more patience and trust in your prayer life? How can you demonstrate a heart of praise and humility in your prayers this week?

LESSON 4
Who and What Should I Pray For?

The Lord is not slow to fulfill his promise as some
count slowness, but is patient toward you,
not wishing that any should perish, but
that all should reach repentance.
2 Peter 3:9 ESV

This is good, and it is pleasing in the sight of God
our Savior, who desires all people to be saved
and to come to the knowledge of the truth.
1 Tim 2:3-4 ESV

Since Adam's fall God's purpose has been to reconcile us to Himself. God's Word emphasizes His concern for the lost — He wants none to perish. This objective was of such critical importance to Him that He sent His Son as an atoning sacrifice. With this in mind, what might you think should be a primary focus of our prayers? Do you realize that there are many unsaved people within your sphere of influence for whom no one is praying? *You may be the only one bringing that name before Almighty God* and you may be the reason that person finally receives God's gift of grace. Pray for the unsaved!

So where should we begin to learn what to pray for? Paul's letters may give us a hint:

Ephesians 1:18 . . . *having the eyes of your __hearts__ enlightened* . . . ESV

1 Thessalonians 3:13 *. . . so that he may establish your __hearts__ blameless in holiness before our God and Father, at the coming of our Lord Jesus with all his saints.* ESV

2 Thessalonians 2:16-17 *Now may our Lord Jesus Christ himself, and God our Father, who loved us and gave us eternal comfort and good hope through grace, 17 comfort your __hearts__ and establish them in every good work and word.* ESV

2 Thessalonians 3:5 *May the Lord direct your __hearts__ to the love of God and to the steadfastness of Christ.* ESV

Our **hearts**! In the context of the ancient world the "heart" was the center of our innermost being. It represented the condition of man. It has a much broader meaning in the Bible than in today's society. A scriptural word study will demonstrate that the heart is the central point for our thinking process, the source of our emotions, and represents our true character.

WHY CONCERN FOR THE HEART?

Genesis 6:5	The thoughts of our hearts are evil.
Jeremiah 17:5	Our hearts turn away from God.
Proverbs 6:16-18	Our hearts devise wicked schemes.
Proverbs 11:20	The Lord hates a perverse heart.
Proverbs 18:12	A man's heart is proud.
Hebrews 3:10	Our hearts are always going astray.
Matthew 15:19	Our hearts produce evil thoughts and actions, like murder and adultery.

These verses certainly make us stop and think. It seems our heart must be right if we are to have any hope of answered prayer. Jesus said, *"Blessed are the pure in heart for they shall see God."* (Matthew 5:8) What about salvation? Does Scripture say anything about our heart and *being saved*?

Question 1: What does Romans 10:9-10 say about the importance of the heart?

Romans 10:9-10 . . . *if you confess with your mouth that Jesus is Lord and believe in your heart that God raised him from the dead, you will be saved. 10 For with the heart one believes and is justified, and with the mouth one confesses and is saved.* ESV

THE GOOD NEWS OF THE GOSPEL

Acts 2:21 *And it shall come to pass that everyone who calls upon the name of the Lord shall be <u>saved</u>.* ESV

1 John 1:9 *If we confess our sins, he is faithful and just to forgive us our sins and to <u>cleanse us</u> from all unrighteousness.* ESV

Romans 10:1 *Brothers, my heart's desire and prayer to God for them is that they <u>may be saved.</u>* ESV

1 Tim 2:1-4 *First of all, then, I urge that supplications, prayers, intercessions, and thanksgivings be made for all people, 2 for kings and all who are in high positions, that we may lead a peaceful and quiet life, godly and dignified in every way. 3 This is good, and it is pleasing in the sight of God our Savior, 4 who desires all people <u>to be saved</u> and to come to the knowledge of the truth.* ESV

Question 2: What three groups above does Timothy instruct us to pray for?

a.

b.

c.

Question 3: Who are people "in authority" that we should pray for?

Question 4: What four things are we are to pray for?

a.

b.

c.

d.

WHO AND WHAT ELSE SHOULD WE PRAY FOR?

Problems:
James 5:13 *Is anyone among you suffering? Let him pray. Is anyone cheerful? Let him sing praise.* ESV

Wisdom:
James 1:5-6 *If any of you lacks wisdom, let him ask God, who gives generously to all without reproach, and it will be given him. 6 But let him ask in faith, with no doubting, for the one who doubts is like a wave of the sea that is driven and tossed by the wind.* ESV

Question 5: How does James 1:5-6 compare with what Solomon asked for in 1 Kings 3:9?

1 Kings 3:9 Give your servant therefore an understanding mind [wisdom] to govern your people, that I may discern between good and evil, for who is able to govern this your great people? ESV

Healing:

James 5:14-16 *Is anyone among you sick? Let him call for the elders of the church, and let them pray over him, anointing him with oil in the name of the Lord. 15 And the prayer of faith will save the one who is sick, and the Lord will raise him up. And if he has committed sins, he will be forgiven. 16 Therefore, confess your sins to one another and pray for one another, that you may be healed. The prayer of a righteous person has great power as it is working.* ESV

Question 6: What are the five requirements above for healing prayer?

1.

2.

3.

4.

5.

City/Country:

Ps 122:6-7 *Pray for the peace of Jerusalem! "May they be secure who love you! 7 Peace be within your walls and security within your towers!"* ESV

Question 7: Do you think we should still pray for the peace of Jerusalem today? Why or why not?

Question 8: Besides Jerusalem, what should we pray for?

Everyone:
Ephesians 6:18 . . . *praying at all times in the Spirit, with all prayer and supplication. To that end keep alert with all perseverance, making supplication for all the saints*. ESV (see also Php 4:6)

Question 9: Who are the "saints"?

Question 10: Does this mean you should pray only for the saints?

Friends:
Luke 22:31-33 *Simon, Simon, behold, Satan demanded to have you, that he might sift you like wheat, 32 but I have prayed for you that your faith may not fail. And when you have turned again, strengthen your brothers*. ESV

Question 11: What often happens when you seriously pray for someone else?

Enemies:
Luke 6:28 *Bless those who curse you, pray for those who abuse you.* ESV

Matthew 5:44 *But I say to you, love your enemies and pray for those who persecute you.* ESV

At first glance praying for your enemies seems impossible. But if our prayer is for their salvation and they come to know the love of Christ, it follows logically that their harsh treatment of us might be reduced or even stopped. Note that the enemies here are the kind who abuse and persecute you!

Evangelists and Pastors:
Matthew 9:38 . . . *therefore pray earnestly to the Lord of the harvest to send out laborers into his harvest."* ESV

This verse tells us to ask God to send workers. This is not necessarily a request for the needs of the workers, although God does want us to honor, support, and encourage those who minister among us. The Apostle Paul consistently asked for prayer in his letters. But he also asked for respect and honor:

1 Thess 5:12-14 *We ask you, brothers, to respect those who labor among you and are over you in the Lord and admonish you, 13 and to esteem them very highly in love because of their work. Be at peace among yourselves.* ESV

Question 12: In the two passages below, underline or highlight where Paul asks for prayer.

Romans 15:30 *I appeal to you, brothers, by our Lord Jesus Christ and by the love of the Spirit, to strive together with me in your prayers to God on my behalf.* ESV

2 Corinthians 1:11 *You also must help us by prayer, so that many will give thanks on our behalf for the blessing granted us through the prayers of many.* ESV

Question 13: In 2 Cor 1:11 above, what is Paul saying about prayer?

Question 14: What does Paul specifically ask we pray for in the following two passages?
Colossians 4:3 *At the same time, pray also for us, that God may open to us a door for the word, to declare the mystery of Christ, on account of which I am in prison.* ESV

Eph 6:19-20 *. . . and also for me, that words may be given to me in opening my mouth boldly to proclaim the mystery of the gospel, 20 for which I am an ambassador in chains, that I may declare it boldly, as I ought to speak.* ESV

WHAT DID PAUL PRAY FOR?
(See Appendix F for Paul's prayers.)

It is very instructive to examine Paul's prayers. It is very interesting to observe that the Bible does not record Paul praying for healing (at least I can't find one). His prayers were focused on personal <u>eternal</u> issues like the condition of our hearts. But also notice how specific Paul is about his prayers. He prays for very specific personal life change.

For example Ephesians 1:17-19 says, *that the God of our Lord Jesus Christ, the Father of glory, may give you a spirit of wisdom and of revelation in the knowledge of him, 18 having the eyes of your hearts enlightened, that you may know what is the hope to which he has called you, what are the riches of his glorious inheritance in the saints, 19 and what is the immeasurable greatness of his power toward us who believe, according to the working of his great might.* ESV

Here we see that Paul prayed:

- for a spirit of wisdom,
- have wisdom and a spirit of revelation of God,
- to know the hope to which we are called, and
- to know the greatness of His power.

Can you imagine how you would feel if Paul had his hand on your shoulder and prayed these words over you?

Then in Colossians 1:9-12 he prayed:

- to be filled with the knowledge of His will,
- to live a life worthy of the Lord,
- to please Him in every way,
- to bear fruit in every good work,
- to grow in the knowledge of God,
- to be strengthened by His power
- to be strengthened with power,
- to have endurance and patience, and
- to joyfully give thanks to the Father.

Unfortunately, we often tend to pray in generalities because we are not sure of God's will and don't really know or perceive what He wants. Then we sometimes feel we are putting God on the spot if we get specific or maybe it becomes easier just to ask for His will to be done. God wants to know what we are asking for. It is also beneficial to us when answers come. The answers can be measured against what we were asking.

Paul also never prayed for shelter, clothing, transportation, food, wealth, or all the things that we need to maintain our lifestyle.

EXERCISE

For each of the passages chosen from Appendix F, choose one request from each prayer that you would like to pray for yourself or someone else. We have provided the last four.

Eph 1:15-23

Eph 3:16-21

Phil 1:3-6

Phil 1:9-11

1 Thes 1:2-3

1 Tim 2:1-2

2 Tim 1:3-4

1 Cor 1:4-9

Col 1:3-6

Col 2:1-3

1 Thes 3:10-13	That my heart will be strengthened so that I would be blameless and holy.
1 Thes 5:16-18	That I will always be joyful.
2 Thes 1:11-12	That He would count me worthy and fulfill every good purpose and plan of mine.
2 Thes 3:1-2	That I would be delivered from wicked and evil men.

What I Want to Remember

Enter some notes and information that you want to remember about this lesson. It might be a Scripture verse or two, something new you learned, something you want to do, something you want to change, or just something you want to be sure to remember.

Wisdom to Action
Challenge

Who are three specific individuals you can commit to interceding for regularly? How can you cultivate a heart that is more deeply concerned for the spiritual well-being of others?

LESSON 5

Why, What, Where, and When Should I Pray?

(Practical Pointers on the Practice of Prayer)

It is only when the whole heart
is gripped with the passion of prayer
that the life-giving fire descends.
E. M. Bounds.[5]

Prayer should not be a legalistic practice that must take place in a certain environment and at a specified time. God is with us and we have direct communion with him whenever we desire to initiate that communication. Jesus says in John 14:13 that he wants to answer our prayers so that *"the Son may bring glory to the Father."* That should be our focus and purpose as well. We should want God's will to be played out in our family, our church, our community, and our nation, so that God is glorified.

DO WE REALLY NEED TO PRAY?

The first draft of this study included looking at several Scriptures like John 15:5 and Jeremiah 33:3 and saying, "Wow!" But in preparing for teaching my first class using these notes I ran across the story of Moses, Aaron, and Hur (Exodus 17:8-13). You might want to read these several verses. I had always seen these verses as a story about brothers helping brothers and a great story to lead into a message based on Eccl 4:9-12: *"Two are better than one . . . a cord of three strands is not quickly broken."*

However, in Exodus 17:11 the author tells us that Moses was on the hill holding up his hands — that is, praying —

and that the battle in the valley with the Amalekites was being won or lost at the place of prayer. The lesson in this passage surely can be about brothers helping brothers, but the more profound message for us is that life's battles are won or lost in the prayer closet and not on the battlefield.

Why do we need to pray? Pray brings God into active participation in our lives. The lesson for the Israelites and us is to understand that we may become weary, we may need the help of an Aaron or Hur in our life, but the ultimate battle is in the heavenly realms of prayer. The battle is spiritual and we need to fight the battle with prayers, seeking the active help of Almighty God.

This story also implies that we may need help praying. We may get tired and need prayer warriors to help hold up our arms (pray). Prayer is hard work and we can become weary if the task is long and hard. We all need people around us like Aaron and Hur who would have our same priorities and would come to our assistance. Again, a cord of three strands is not easily broken. Paul himself, a great man of prayer asked his brothers to pray:

> *I appeal to you, brothers, by our Lord Jesus Christ*
> *and by the love of the Spirit, to strive together*
> *with me in your prayers to God on my behalf,*
> Romans 15:30 ESV

Question 1: Can you recall an experience in your life when God didn't seem to solve or fix a problem until you began praying? What happened?

Maybe the most important reason to pray is that John 5:5 says we can do nothing apart from God. We need to be holding onto the Vine, otherwise, we have no ability or power to do His work. Yes, we might do something, but it will not be what His power would produce. The spirit is willing but the body is weak (Mt 26:41). Then there is another amazing reason:

He will tell us great and unsearchable things!
Jeremiah 33:3

WHAT SHOULD WE PRAY FOR?

We will revisit this question again briefly, even though we covered this subject in Lesson #4, but we want to consider several other Scriptures. Remember that Philippians 4:6 says, "*do not be anxious about anything, but in everything by prayer and supplication with thanksgiving let your requests be made known to God.*" ESV

Question 2: Do you think Philippians 4:6 really means everything? If yes, then should athletes pray to win games? Should you pray for business success? What do you think God means by "everything?"

WHAT DOES THE LORD'S PRAYER SUGGEST WE PRAY?

Luke 11:2-4 *And he said to them, "When you pray, say: "Father, hallowed be your name. Your kingdom come. 3 Give us each day our daily bread,4 and forgive us our sins, for we ourselves forgive everyone who is indebted to us. And lead us not into temptation."* ESV

Question 3: What four needs does the Lord's Prayer tell us to pray for?

1.

2.

3.

4.

Jesus himself has told us exactly how we are to pray. First, recognize who we are praying to (the heavenly Father), then praise His attributes (His name is hallowed); pray for His kingdom to come on this earth (as it is in heaven where He is the exalted King of kings and Lord of lords); ask for your daily needs (food, clothes and shelter — needs, not wants); ask forgiveness for your sins (and don't withhold forgiveness from those who sin against you); ask Him to protect you from evil and to help you resist the world's temptations, and then praise Him again for His kingdom, His power, the gift of His Holy Spirit, and the gift of His Son who gave us eternal life. Close your prayer asking that His will be done in your life so that He is glorified.

If you have time and are interested, compare the Lord's Prayer in Matthew 6 with Jesus' prayer in John 17. Note the similarities and the differences in subject matter. Also notice who Jesus prays for in John 17: Himself, His disciples, and all believers, including all future believers.

Notes:

God's Word outlines many people and concerns for prayer. Sometimes these subjects can seem very generic or impersonal. But God's Word also tells us of some very specific personal life conditions to pray for. Look up the specific prayer requests in the following two passages:

Ephesians 3:16-19

1.

2.

3.

4.

5.

Colossians 1:9-12

1.

2.

3.

4.

5.

6.

7.

8.

Question 4: Why do you think it is important to pray as specifically as possible?

Question 5: Why do we tend to pray in generalities?

IS LOCATION IMPORTANT?

Question 6: What do the following Scriptures suggest regarding prayer?

Mark 11:17 *And he was teaching them and saying to them, "Is it not written, 'My house shall be called a house of prayer for all the nations'? But you have made it a den of robbers." ESV*

Matthew 6:6 *But when you pray, go into your room and shut the door and pray to your Father who is in secret. And your Father who sees in secret will reward you. ESV*

Luke 5:16 *But he would withdraw to desolate places and pray. ESV*

Matt 18:19-20 *Again I say to you, if two of you agree on earth about anything they ask, it will be done for them by my Father in heaven. 20 For where two or three are gathered in my name, there am I among them. ESV*

Mk 11:17

Mt 6:6

Lk 5:16

Mt 18: 19-20

Although the teaching in Matthew 6:6 is very clear about praying alone in private, it is only in reference to corporate prayer in Mt 18:19 (with two or three) that the promise is added that, "it will be done for you." We can logically conclude that God recognizes a special or unique power in corporate prayer.

Often when we begin interceding (praying seriously) for another person we become very invested in that need. A new and deeper relationship can develop. We may tend to be more gracious or begin to treat the person as a friend. We can also begin to be part of the solution.

Question 7: What other things tend to happen when we undertake serious prayer for another person?

Question 8: Mt 18:20 adds that Jesus "is among" those gathered in prayer corporately. Do you think this is literally true?

Question 9: But what is unique about this promise?

Question 10: Why is it often difficult for people to pray publically or corporately?

Question 11: What does "gathered in my name" (Mt 18:20) mean or imply?

IS MY PRAYER POSITION IMPORTANT?

Record in Question 12 below the different prayer positions described in the following passages.

Genesis 18:22 *So the men turned from there and went toward Sodom, but Abraham still stood before the Lord.* ESV

Mark 11:25 *And whenever you stand praying, forgive, if you have anything against anyone, so that your Father also who is in heaven may forgive you your trespasses.* ESV

Exodus 34:8 *And Moses quickly bowed his head toward the earth and worshiped.* ESV

Joshua 7:6 *Then Joshua tore his clothes and fell to the earth on his face before the ark of the Lord until the evening, he and the elders of Israel. And they put dust on their heads.* ESV

Matthew 26:39 *And going a little farther he fell on his face and prayed, saying, "My Father, if it be possible, let this cup pass from me; nevertheless, not as I will, but as you will." ESV*

1 Kings 8:54 *Now as Solomon finished offering all this prayer and plea to the Lord, he arose from before the altar of the Lord, where he had knelt with hands outstretched toward heaven. ESV*

Luke 22:41 *And he withdrew from them about a stone's throw, and knelt down and prayed, ESV*

2 Chronicles 6:12 *Then Solomon stood before the altar of the Lord in the presence of all the assembly of Israel and spread out his hands. ESV*

1 Timothy 2:8 *I desire then that in every place the men should pray, lifting holy hands without anger or quarreling; ESV*

Exodus 9:29 *Moses said to him, "As soon as I have gone out of the city, I will stretch out my hands to the Lord. The thunder will cease, and there will be no more hail, so that you may know that the earth is the Lord's." ESV*

Question 12: What are the different prayer positions reported in the above verses?

Genesis 18:22

Mark 11:25

Exodus 34:8

Joshua 7:6

Matthew 26:39

1 Kings 8:54

Luke 22:41

2 Chronicles 6:12

1 Timothy 2:8

Exodus 9:29

It seems clear that there is no single specific position for prayer. If you have never knelt for prayer, I would ask you why? You may never have felt like prostrating yourself, but have you never felt humbled enough to the point of kneeling? Think about it!

WHEN SHOULD WE PRAY?

Question 13: When did Jesus often pray?

Mark 1:35 *And rising very early in the morning, while it was still dark, he departed and went out to a desolate place, and there he prayed.* ESV

Question 14: Other than the possibility that Jesus was a "morning person," why should morning be better than evening?

Question 15: What do you think Paul means by praying "without ceasing" in 1 Thessalonians 5:17?
1 Thess 5:17-18 *pray without ceasing, 18 give thanks in all circumstances; for this is the will of God in Christ Jesus for you.* ESV

It is interesting to observe that Daniel prayed three time a day (Daniel 6:10). One might wonder or think that means we should pray in that manner. The context in Daniel indicates that he was serious about his prayer life and in his faith and obedience to God. He wasn't about to stop praying to his God just because the king had decreed it illegal. He was determined and committed. It seems more logical and reasonable to assume the three times per day was a cultural practice or simply how Daniel chose to schedule his prayer time. I believe it is praying regularly and diligently that is being suggested.

OBSTACLES TO PRAYING

There are various reasons or obstacles that individuals may cite for failing to pray regularly. Some are valid and some are merely excuses. If you do not perceive value in praying or being more intimate with God, it is very difficult to set any time aside to pray. Otherwise your prayer time is often limited to saying grace and praying for relief when something bad happens.

Some of the most common obstacles to an effective prayer life are:

Busyness: You may feel overwhelmed with responsibilities, commitments, and distractions, which cause you to prioritize other activities over prayer.

Time management: You may struggle with time management and prioritization, failing to allocate sufficient time for prayer because of other demands for your time.

Prayer is hard work: Prayer not only takes time but it requires some thought and understanding about real needs. This can be mentally and emotionally challenging, particularly if the situation is difficult or heart-breaking. It can also encourage you to be part of the solution and that may be frightening. It can cause you to take on the stress and pain of others, which may be exhausting.

Distractions: In today's fast-paced world it can be challenging to maintain focus and concentration during your prayer time. External distractions such as noise, phone notifications, and personal obligations can hinder a person's ability to engage. It is easy for your mind to revert to your plans for the day, especially if the day is important or you have something you love or want to do.

Apathy: You may be going through a period of spiritual dryness and you are struggling to connect with God because He feels distant.

Self-discipline: Maintaining a consistent prayer life requires discipline and intentionality. You may find it difficult to establish and maintain a regular prayer routine.

Self-reliance: You may want to rely more on your own abilities and resources rather than turning to God in prayer. This can lead to neglecting prayer and even rejecting any dependence on God. This often occurs when you are very successful in the world. Remember what was said about the rich man and the eye of the needle. You many feel you don't really need God's help and you would prefer to trust yourself rather than God.

Unbelief: Doubts or skepticism about the importance or significance of prayer can deter you from engaging in regular prayer. If you doubt whether prayer makes a difference or if God will respond, you are likely to consider it a waste of valuable time.

Guilt or shame: Feelings of guilt or shame over past failures, mistakes, or sins can create a barrier to prayer. You may feel unworthy or hesitant to approach God, fearing His judgment or disapproval.

Fear: Opening up to God in prayer requires vulnerability and transparency. You may fear being vulnerable with God or struggle with the intimacy required to express your emotions and needs.

Past history: Past disappointments, unanswered prayers, or negative religious experiences may lead to disillusionment and doubt. You may be very discouraged or disappointed in how God has chosen to answer or not answer your prayers. Thus, you have lost any motivation or interest in praying.

Lack of knowledge and understanding: You may lack understanding or training in prayer. Not knowing how to pray effectively or feeling uncertain about what to pray can often hinder your prayer life.

Addressing these obstacles often involves intentional effort, self-reflection, and reliance on God's grace. Overcoming barriers to prayer may require making adjustments to your schedule, seeking support from fellow believers, or renewing your relationship with God.

THOUGHT QUESTIONS

1. How important is prayer in your life? Why? Is it a daily priority or only used for emergencies?

2. Have you committed time to prayer? How much?

3. What characteristics of effective prayer need to be implemented in your life?

4. Do you presently have a serious roadblock in your prayer life? What's it going to take to overcome that roadblock?

What I Want to Remember

Enter some notes and information that you want to remember about this lesson. It might be a Scripture verse or two, something new you learned, something you want to do, something you want to change, or just something you want to be sure to remember.

Wisdom to Action
Challenge

How can you integrate more moments of prayer throughout your day? What areas of your life do you need to surrender more fully to God's will and glory?

LESSON 6
What Results Can I Expect?

Now to him who is able to do far more abundantly
than all that we ask or think, according to the
power at work within us.
Ephesians 3:20 ESV

If we want results we need to know that God hears us.
Does God hear the prayers of everyone? What about the
prayers of unbelievers and sinners? Does God hear their
prayers? Will He hear us during times that we are
unrepentant? Let's examine first what Scripture says about
God hearing our prayers.

DOES GOD HEAR OUR PRAYERS?

Review the following verses for God's promise to hear us.
Underline or highlight where it says or implied God heard.
Then record what it says about how the one involved
acted as a result of God hearing. We have underlined the
first passage for you.

2 Kings 22:19 . . . *because your heart was penitent, and
you humbled yourself before the Lord, when you heard
how I spoke against this place and against its inhabitants,
that they should become a desolation and a curse, and you
have torn your clothes and wept before me, <u>I also have
heard you</u>, declares the Lord.* ESV

Psalms 10:17 *O Lord, you hear the desire of the afflicted; you will strengthen their heart; you will incline your ear.* ESV

Psalms 34:15, 17 *The eyes of the Lord are toward the righteous and his ears toward their cry. . . . 17 When the righteous cry for help, the Lord hears and delivers them out of all their troubles.* ESV

Psalms 40:1 *I waited patiently for the Lord; he inclined to me and heard my cry.* ESV

Ps 65:1-2 *Praise is due to you, O God, in Zion, and to you shall vows be performed. 2 O you who hears prayer, to you shall all flesh come.* ESV

1 Peter 3:12 *For the eyes of the Lord are on the righteous, and his ears are open to their prayer. But the face of the Lord is against those who do evil.* ESV

1 John 5:14-15 *And this is the confidence that we have toward him, that if we ask anything according to his will he hears us. 15 And if we know that he hears us in whatever we ask, we know that we have the requests that we have asked of him.* ESV

It is clear from these Scriptures that God does hear prayer. **But notice** that in every case Scripture associates an important characteristic or requirement for the one who is praying. It does not say directly that these characteristics are required for God to hear and act, but the inference is very strong that is the case. If we want God to do what we ask it is only logical that we must do what He asks.

DOES GOD EVER <u>NOT</u> HEAR OR LISTEN?

Surprisingly, the answer to the question in the heading is yes. Not surprisingly the basic problem is sin and disobedience. In the Old Testament, Isaiah says it very bluntly:

Isaiah 59:2 *. . . but your iniquities have made a separation between you and your God, and your sins have hidden his face from you so that <u>he does not hear</u>.* ESV

Throughout the Old Testament there are a number of verses that speak to the issue of God not listening or not hearing. In Isaiah 1:15 the problem is idolatry and evil; in Proverbs 21:13 the problem is the result of not helping the poor. Using your Bible, look up Hosea 5:3-7 and list the six reasons that when, "they seek the Lord, they will not find him" because "he has withdrawn from them."

1.

2.

3.

4.

5.

6.

In the New Testament John states the position very clearly:

John 9:31 *We know that God does not listen to sinners, but if anyone is a worshiper of God and does his will, God listens to him.* ESV

Question 1: We know that we are all sinners, so what does it mean that God will not listen to sinners?

Question 2: How is it possible for a God who is everywhere present (omnipresent) not to hear or listen to our prayers?

Question 3: In Lesson 3, what was the underlying problem that caused prayers not to be answered?

WHAT RESULTS MIGHT WE EXPECT?

First and foremost we must not forget the following:

Joel 2:32 *And it shall come to pass that everyone who calls on the name of the Lord shall be saved. For in Mount Zion and in Jerusalem there shall be those who escape, as the Lord has said, and among the survivors shall be those whom the Lord calls.* ESV

Remember the meaning of "name." It refers to the entirety or totality of God. God wants to meet our needs. Here it is those calling on His name who "shall be saved."

In Matthew 7:9 and 11 Jesus paints a graphic example of why God can and will do immeasurably more than we need.

Matthew 7:9, 11 *Or which one of you, if his son asks him for bread, will give him a stone? . . . 11 If you then, who are evil, know how to give good gifts to your children, how much more will your Father who is in heaven give good things to those who ask him!* ESV

Question 4a. Record what results might be expected based on the following Scriptures:

Ps 118:5-6 *Out of my distress I called on the Lord; the Lord answered me and set me free. 6 The Lord is on my side; I will not fear. What can man do to me?* ESV

Psalms 138:3 *On the day I called, you answered me; my strength of soul you increased.* ESV

Isa 58:9-11 *Then you shall call, and the Lord will answer; you shall cry, and he will say, 'Here I am.' If you take away the yoke from your midst, the pointing of the finger, and speaking wickedness, 10 if you pour yourself out for the hungry and satisfy the desire of the afflicted, then shall your light rise in the darkness and your gloom be as the noonday. 11 And the Lord will guide you continually and satisfy your desire in scorched places and make your bones strong; and you shall be like a watered garden, like a spring of water, whose waters do not fail. ESV*

Look at the last two sentences above in Isa 58 10-11. Think about what this would have meant to the Israelite living in a barren land.

Dan 9:22-23 *He made me understand, speaking with me and saying, "O Daniel, I have now come out to give you insight and understanding. 23 At the beginning of your pleas for mercy a word went out, and I have come to tell it to you, for you are greatly loved. Therefore consider the word and understand the vision. ESV*

Matthew 6:6 *But when you pray, go into your room and shut the door and pray to your Father who is in secret. And your Father who sees in secret will reward you. ESV*

Question 4b: Does Mt 6:6 mean we will receive answers to prayer, or that we receive additional rewards? [The translation of the New American Standard Version for "reward" is "repay." For further understanding, look at the context of Matthew 6]

Question 5: What does it mean in John 16:23-24 that Jesus says, "Until now you have not asked for anything in my name"?
John 16:23-24   *In that day you will ask nothing of me. Truly, truly, I say to you, whatever you ask of the Father in my name, he will give it to you. 24 Until now you have asked nothing in my name. Ask, and you will receive, that your joy may be full.* ESV

Question 6: What does the "peace of God" imply in Php 4:6-7?
Philippians 4:6-7 *. . . do not be anxious about anything, but in everything by prayer and supplication with thanksgiving let your requests be made known to God. 7 And the peace of God, which surpasses all understanding, will guard your hearts and your minds in Christ Jesus.* ESV

Question 7: What is to be our focus based on 2 Corinthians 4:16-18?

2 Corinthians 4:16-18 *So we do not lose heart. Though our outer nature is wasting away, our inner nature is being renewed day by day. 17 For this slight momentary affliction is preparing for us an eternal weight of glory beyond all comparison, 18 as we look not to the things that are seen but to the things that are unseen. For the things that are seen are transient, but the things that are unseen are eternal.* ESV

Question 8: What does 1 Peter 5:7 say we are to do about anxiety?

1 Peter 5:7 *. . . casting all your anxieties on him, because he cares for you.* ESV

Question 9: What three things does Matthew 6:25-34 tell us not to worry about, and why?

1.

2.

3.

One way to be anxious about nothing is to pray about everything. Fix your eyes on what is eternal and know that God will answer. Put it in God's hands. E.M. Bounds addresses the question of God answering prayer in a very realistic and logical manner:

"To answer prayer is God's universal rule . . . God's Word does not say, 'Call onto me and you will thereby be trained into the happy art of knowing how to be denied. Ask, and you will learn sweet patience by getting nothing.' Far from it. But it is definite, clear and positive: 'Ask, and it shall be given unto you.'"[6]

MEDITATION

We have an awesome God! Think back over the past six lessons about His promises in relationship to prayer. Has God ever not kept a promise? Have you ever doubted God's presence because He didn't answer a prayer? Meditate on one or more of the following:

Numbers 23:19 *God is not man, that he should lie, or a son of man, that he should change his mind. Has he said, and will he not do it? Or has he spoken, and will he not fulfill it?* ESV

Psalms 86:5 *For you, O Lord, are good and forgiving, abounding in steadfast love to all who call upon you.* ESV

Isaiah 65:24 *Before they call I will answer; while they are yet speaking I will hear.* ESV

1 Peter 4:19 *Therefore let those who suffer according to God's will entrust their souls to a faithful Creator while doing good.* ESV

1 Corinthians 10:13 *No temptation has overtaken you that is not common to man. God is faithful, and he will not let you be tempted beyond your ability, but with the temptation he will also provide the way of escape, that you may be able to endure it.* ESV

Question 10: Which of the passages above is most meaningful to you? Why?

DISCUSSION QUESTIONS

1. What is the most fantastic answer to prayer God has ever given you, or your family?

2. Examine what Psalm 34:15-19 says: He watches over the righteous, protects from evil, hears, delivers, saves, protects, and redeems. What more do you want or need from God?

3. Why must 1 Peter 4:19 above be true?

4. What are the requirements for receiving God's help in the following verses?

Ps 86:5

1 Peter 4:19

1 Cor 10:13

What I Want to Remember

Enter some notes and information that you want to remember about this lesson. It might be a Scripture verse or two, something new you learned, something you want to do, something you want to change, or just something you want to be sure to remember.

Wisdom to Action
Challenge

Reflect on a recent prayer experience. How did it impact your relationship with God? What can you do to make your prayer times more transformative encounters with Him?

LESSON 7
Praying With Boldness
The Prayer of Jabez

"Fortune favors the bold."
Virgil

"Boldness be my friend."
William Shakespeare

There are only two verses in the Bible that mention Jabez, but they have important lessons to teach us:

- It is acceptable to pray for blessings for yourself.
- It hints as to why God answered this prayer.
- It suggests our motives and how we could pray.
- It makes us consider if our prayers are big enough.

THE SCRIPTURE

Some translations translate the fourth prayer request in this passage, "*so that it might not bring me pain*"(ESV), as a request not to cause pain to someone else. Both interpretations are reasonable given the original text, but they provide different perspectives. The HCSB and NKJV below provide this latter interpretation in comparison with the ESV.

1 Chronicles 4:9-10   ESV
Jabez was more honorable than his brothers; and his mother called his name Jabez, saying, "Because I bore him in pain." 10 Jabez called upon the God of Israel, saying, "Oh that you would bless me and enlarge my border, and

that your hand might be with me, and that you would keep me from harm so that it might not bring me pain!" And God granted what he asked.

1 Chronicles 4:9-10   HCSB
Jabez was more honorable than his brothers. His mother named him Jabez and said, "I gave birth to him in pain." 10 Jabez called out to the God of Israel: "If only You would bless me, extend my border, let Your hand be with me, and keep me from harm, so that I will not cause any pain." And God granted his request.

1 Chronicles 4:9-10   NKJV
Now Jabez was more honorable than his brothers, and his mother called his name Jabez, saying, "Because I bore him in pain." 10 And Jabez called on the God of Israel saying, "Oh, that You would bless me indeed, and enlarge my territory, that Your hand would be with me, and that You would keep me from evil, that I may not cause pain!" So God granted him what he requested.

THE CONTEXT

This passage occurs in the middle of a series of genealogies describing the ancestry of the Hebrew nation. The first two chapters in 1 Chronicles trace the Israelites' history from Adam through Caleb's sons. Chapter 3 describes David's descendants and Chapter 4 lists other descendants of Judah. It's here that we find Jabez. In general no information is given other than the names linked to the parents. This is the only place in the Bible Jabez or his prayer is mentioned.

WHAT DO WE KNOW?

The passage says that Jabez was more honorable than his brothers, but it does not explain what that means. It also tells us that he was birthed in pain but there is no explanation of that statement either.

We are simply told of a prayer Jabez prayed:

- He asked to be blessed.
- He asked that his border [or *territory*] be enlarged, meaning an increase of his wealth and influence.
- He asked that God's hand to be upon him; that is, God's protection and empowerment.
- He asked that he would be protected from harm and pain, or that he would not cause pain.

Lastly, and perhaps most importantly, we are told that God granted his requests. These are very straightforward prayer requests. One might think that asking for blessing is presumptuous, but apparently God found it acceptable as the text tells us He granted the request. Since the first request, "bless me," is very general, it is reasonable to look at the remainder of the requests as specific ways in which he wishes to be blessed.

IMPLICATIONS AND OBSERVATIONS

First and foremost in making any observations about this prayer and its implications, since God answered the prayer, we should assume that the prayer was acceptable and appropriate, at least for the time and place involved.

Given the fact that God granted Jabez's requests, what might we assume about the requests? First, blessings are available and God will grant them. Second, wealth and power are not inherently bad, and God is willing to grant them to those He chooses. Third, He will empower us in some or in many areas of our lives, but we may need to ask. Fourth, pain and evil are real and we need protection from them.

Finally, we need to pray with the right motives. Jabez did not wish to be harmed or cause harm that might result in pain in his life or the life of another. Having the right motive is also confirmed in the New Testament:

You ask and do not receive, because you ask wrongly,
to spend it on your passions. James 4:3 ESV

There are two hints in this passage as to why God might have chosen to answer this prayer:

- Jabez was more honorable, and
- He asked God to prevent him from causing pain (HCSB and NKJV).

If the HCSB and NKJV translations are closer to the correct interpretation, we observe a humble spirit in his desire not to cause pain to others. Obviously God knows Jabez's heart and in the end, that may determine whether God is going to answer a prayer of this nature.

DISCUSSION QUESTIONS

1. Why would God want this extra information about Jabez in the genealogies? What makes his prayer worthy of mention?

2. What do <u>you</u> think it means that Jebez was "more honorable than his brothers"?

3. How can we pray this prayer and not be selfish? What should be our <u>motives</u>?

4. When <u>you</u> ask for blessing what are <u>you</u> personally thinking you are asking for? What are you expecting?

5. Territory (land) was a fundamental wealth component during the time of Jabez. If you were praying a similar prayer today, what might you pray for? Why?

6. If "territory" represents relationships, in what ways do you think God might want you to enlarge your personal territory? Why?

7. What would your life look like if God poured out His blessing on you and your family? In what areas of your life would He be most likely to bless you? Why?

8. Was there ever a time in <u>your</u> life when you asked for God's power? What happened?

9. What are some of the excuses we all give for staying in our comfort zones instead of praying boldly?

10. What evil do you want God to protect you from? Are there areas of your life that you play close to the edge where you need God's power to keep you safe?

11. What, if anything, are <u>you</u> doing today that requires God's power, other than life in general?

12. What do you think constitutes a bold prayer?

13. Are your prayers big enough? Do your prayers have eternal significance?

EXERCISE

Expand one or more of the sections of Jabez's prayer. Rewrite the prayer so that it is personal, in modern terms, and adds substance to your requests. We have expanded the first request. Do at least one of the others for yourself.

"Bless Me"
Lord, I desire Your blessing! Please pour out in my life every possible blessing You desire for me. Father, I want You working in my life and I need the guidance and direction of the Holy Spirit so that my walk is pleasing to You. Bless me so that I can be a blessing to others. I desire Your blessing so that You receive honor and thanksgiving from others who see You working in my life. Bless me O Lord. AMEN.

Expanded Prayer

Subject:

My Prayer:

What I Want to Remember

Enter some notes and information that you want to remember about this lesson. It might be a Scripture verse or two, something new you learned, something you want to do, something you want to change, or just something you want to be sure to remember.

Wisdom to Action
Challenge

What bold request, aligned with God's will and focused on honoring Him, can you commit to praying for consistently over the next month?

LESSON 8
How is Fasting Related to Prayer

"Fasting cleanses the soul, raises the mind, subjects one's flesh to the spirit, renders the heart contrite and humble, scatters the clouds of concupiscence, quenches the fire of lust, and kindles the true light of chastity."
Augustine of Hippo

Fasting is best described as giving up something important for some period of time, usually determined in advance. The item given up is usually food but it could be TV, alcohol, smoking, reading, sexual relations, sports, or anything that tends to be important in your life.

WHAT IS THE PURPOSE OF FASTING?

Religious fasting should be directed at either (1) elevating the presence of God in your life (coming closer to God), or (2) a very specific spiritual purpose (perhaps some sin in your life) or some need in the church.

Fasting brings urgency, priority, resolution, importance, and seriousness to our praying and gives it a force and power in the heavenly realms. Fasting is a powerful weapon against spiritual decay because it requires us to focus on God.

God asks us to humble ourselves (Matthew 18:4; 23:12; James 4:10 and 1 Peter 5:6). I believe an examination of Scripture will determine that *one* important way to do that is through fasting. It is not the *only* way, but one that is clearly outlined in Scripture (Leviticus 16:29-31; Psalm 35:13; Ezra 8:21). God clearly <u>required</u> fasting under Old Testament doctrine. But what does the New Testament say about fasting?

JESUS HIMSELF FASTED

We should observe that Luke reports that Jesus fasted:

Luke 4:1-2 *And Jesus, full of the Holy Spirit, returned from the Jordan and was led by the Spirit in the wilderness 2 for forty days, being tempted by the devil. And he ate nothing during those days. And when they were ended, he was hungry.* ESV

Question 1: Why would Jesus fast at this time?

JESUS' TEACHING

Jesus discussed fasting with His disciples:

Matt 6:17-18 *But when you fast, anoint your head and wash your face, 18 that your fasting may not be seen by others but by your Father who is in secret. And your Father who sees in secret will reward you.* ESV

Luke 5:35 *The days will come when the bridegroom is taken away from them, and then they will fast in those days.* ESV

Question 2: What conditions or restraints does Jesus place on fasting?

Question 3: Does Jesus expect the church to fast?

THE EARLY CHURCH

Acts 13:2-3 *While they were worshiping the Lord and fasting, the Holy Spirit said, "Set apart for me Barnabas and Saul for the work to which I have called them." 3 Then after fasting and praying they laid their hands on them and sent them off.* ESV

Acts 14:23 *And when they had appointed elders for them in every church, with prayer and fasting they committed them to the Lord in whom they had believed.* ESV

Question 4: When did the early church fast and for what purpose?

In general, today's church has given up the discipline of fasting. I believe that this is a grave mistake of the church. Our purpose here is to examine how and where fasting is associated with prayer. Our subject in this book is prayer, not fasting, but is there a special or unique relationship between these two disciplines? Notice in the two verses from Acts (above) that the early church prayed _and_ fasted.

PRAYER AND FASTING IN THE OLD TESTAMENT

In the first verse below you will note a reference to "sackcloth and ashes." Sackcloth and ashes were often used as a public confession and repentance mechanism. Since this reference occurs frequently in the Scriptures related to fasting, the following definitions should be helpful:

> *Sackcloth:* a loose cloth (often coarse or mesh-like) made of goat's hair (Isaiah 50:3). It was used for sacks and for the garments of mourners (Genesis 37:34). It might be worn next to the skin in extreme cases, but was usually worn or draped over the shoulders as an outer garment or coat.

> *Ashes:* often employed by mourners as a symbol of grief and mourning (Isaiah 58:5; Jeremiah 6:26) by either sitting in ashes or scattering them over the shoulders or entire body.[7]

Note the following passages indicating that the people both prayed <u>and</u> fasted. We have underlined the reference to fasting and prayer for your convenience.

> **Daniel 9:3** *Then I turned my face to the Lord God, seeking him by <u>prayer and pleas for mercy with fasting</u> and sackcloth and ashes.* ESV

> **Joel 1:14** <u>*Consecrate a fast*</u>*; call a solemn assembly. Gather the elders and all the inhabitants of the land to the house of the Lord your God, and <u>cry out to the Lord</u>.* ESV

> **2 Chronicles 7:14** *if my people who are called by my name <u>Humble themselves, and pray and seek my face</u> and turn from their wicked ways, then I will hear from heaven and will forgive their sin and heal their land.* ESV
>
> **NOTE:** Scripture does not say or imply what the people should do to humble themselves. Fasting may be one possibility but it does not say that directly here. Note Psalms 69:10 and Ezra 8:21.

Ezra 8:23 So <u>we fasted</u> and <u>implored our God for this</u>, and he listened to our entreaty.

Nehemiah 1:4 *As soon as I heard these words I sat down and <u>wept and mourned for days, and I continued fasting and praying before the God of heaven</u>.* ESV

Jonah 3:5-6, 8 *And the people of Nineveh believed God. <u>They called for a fast and put on sackcloth</u>, from the greatest of them to the least of them. 6 The word reached the king of Nineveh, and he arose from his throne, removed his robe, covered himself with sackcloth, and <u>sat in ashes</u>. . . . . 8 but let man and beast be covered with sackcloth, and <u>let them call out mightily to God</u>. Let everyone turn from his evil way and from the violence that is in his hands.* ESV

Psalms 35:12-13 *They repay me evil for good; my soul is bereft. 13 But I, when they were sick—I wore sackcloth; <u>I afflicted myself with fasting; I prayed with head bowed on my chest</u>.* ESV

Esther 4:15-5:3 contains a special story about fasting. Even though prayer is not specifically mentioned, it seems obvious that the time of weeping, mourning and fasting was accompanied by prayer. The result was that the Jewish people were not annihilated. This victory is still celebrated by the Jews as the Feast of Purim.

All of the above examples occur in periods of extreme need or when dire events required God's help. When man was incapable of solving the problem, God's intervention was absolutely necessary, and the crying out to God in prayer was accompanied by fasting. I believe the church must take to heart Jesus' response to the question about fasting:

Luke 5:33-35 *And they said to him, "The disciples of John fast often and offer prayers, and so do the disciples of the Pharisees, but yours eat and drink." 34 And Jesus said to*

them, "Can you make wedding guests fast while the bridegroom is with them? 35 The days will come when the bridegroom is taken away from them, and then they will fast in those days." ESV

DO THE SCRIPTURES EVER SPEAK AGAINST FASTING?

Jeremiah 14:11-12 *The Lord said to me: "Do not pray for the welfare of this people. 12 Though they fast, I will not hear their cry, and though they offer burnt offering and grain offering, I will not accept them. But I will consume them by the sword, by famine, and by pestilence." ESV*

Question 5: Why do you think this is God's position? Is this consistent with His character?
[After thinking about your answer, look at Jeremiah 14:10]

PROBLEMS AND ABUSES!

There can be problems with fasting. Any practice can be used for the wrong purposes. Do not conclude that the practice is bad simply because some use it improperly or for the wrong reasons. Let's look at four problems identified in Scripture.

PROBLEM: Ritual

Galatians 5:18 *But if you are led by the Spirit, you are not under the law. ESV*

Colossians 2:20-23 *If with Christ you died to the elemental spirits of the world, why, as if you were still alive in the world, do you submit to regulations— 21 "Do not handle,*

Do not taste, Do not touch" 22 (referring to things that all perish as they are used)—according to human precepts and teachings? 23 These have indeed an appearance of wisdom in promoting self-made religion and asceticism and severity to the body, but they are of no value in stopping the indulgence of the flesh. ESV

Question 6: Given the verses above, what conclusions can you draw about a strict ritual of fasting (e.g. every Tuesday)?

Although the New Testament church is under no Scriptural doctrine to fast (except as led by the Spirit) personal and corporate fasting are certainly appropriate, particularly if called by church leaders or elders. But long, permanent, or regular and ritualistic fasting is not consistent with Scripture.

PROBLEM: Purpose

Isaiah 58:3-5 *'Why have we fasted, and you see it not? Why have we humbled ourselves, and you take no knowledge of it?' Behold, in the day of your fast you seek your own pleasure, and oppress all your workers. 4 Behold, you fast only to quarrel and to fight and to hit with a wicked fist. Fasting like yours this day will not make your voice to be heard on high. 5 Is such the fast that I choose, a day for a person to humble himself? Is it to bow down his head like a reed, and to spread sackcloth and ashes under him? Will you call this a fast, and a day acceptable to the Lord?* ESV

Question 7: What were the people in Isaiah 58:3-5 trying to do?

We must know the purpose for our fasting and it should be accompanied with right living. Our fasting will have little impact on God if we are living sinful lives.

PROBLEM: Pride

Luke 18:11-12 *The Pharisee, standing by himself, prayed thus: 'God, I thank you that I am not like other men, extortioners, unjust, adulterers, or even like this tax collector. 12 I fast twice a week; I give tithes of all that I get.'* ESV

Question 8: What was the Pharisee doing? Why?

PROBLEM: Focus:

Matthew 6:16-18 *And when you fast, do not look gloomy like the hypocrites, for they disfigure their faces that their fasting may be seen by others. . . . so that your fasting may not be seen by others but by your Father who is in secret. And your Father who sees in secret will reward you.* ESV

Zechariah 7:5-6 *Say to all the people of the land and the priests, When you fasted and mourned in the fifth month and in the seventh, for these seventy years, was it for me that you fasted? 6 And when you eat and when you drink, do you not eat for yourselves and drink for yourselves?* ESV

Question 9: Who is the focus in the above passages? Who should be the focus?

Question 10: Based on the following passages, who or what should be the focus of our fasting?

Isaiah 58:6-7 *Is not this the fast that I choose: to loose the bonds of wickedness, to undo the straps of the yoke,to let the oppressed go free, and to break every yoke? 7 Is it not to share your bread with the hungry and bring the homeless poor into your house; when you see the naked, to cover him, and not to hide yourself from your own flesh?* ESV
Philippians 2:3-4 *Do nothing from rivalry or conceit, but in humility count others more significant than yourselves. 4 Let each of you look not only to his own interests, but also to the interests of others.* ESV

DISCUSSION QUESTION: What issue might you or your church determine is important enough to warrant fasting? Why?

THOUGHT QUESTION: What is so important in your life that if you gave it up for a week, God would be pleased because He knew you were serious?

What I Want to Remember

Enter some notes and information that you want to remember about this lesson. It might be a Scripture verse or two, something new you learned, something you want to do, something you want to change, or just something you want to be sure to remember.

Wisdom to Action
Challenge

Consider incorporating a day of fasting and prayer this month. What specific spiritual need or area of growth will you focus on during this time?

LESSON 9
What should be the purpose of our fast?

"Fasting is a means of discipline and self-denial,
a way of focusing our attention
on God and His will."
Dietrich Bonhoeffer

We should agree, based on Lesson 8, that the New Testament church is called to fast and that fasting and prayer go hand in hand, particularly when a situation is desperate. The words "fast," "fasting," and "fasted" appear the in Bible approximately 130 times.

When did the Old Testament saints and early church fast? Why did they fast? What were their purposes? What can we learn by examining the past that would be helpful today?

PURPOSE: Fasting to come closer to God.

The following Scriptures outline reasons for fasting that in general indicate that the purpose is to come closer to God in some way. Record the specific reasons for the fasts in each passage below:

Ezra 8:23 *So we fasted and implored our God for this, and he listened to our entreaty.* ESV

Matthew 4:1-2 *Then Jesus was led up by the Spirit into the wilderness to be tempted by the devil. 2 And after fasting forty days and forty nights, he was hungry.* ESV

Joel 2:12 *"Yet even now," declares the Lord, "return to me with all your heart, with fasting, with weeping, and with mourning.* ESV

Psalms 69:10 *When I wept and humbled my soul with fasting, it became my reproach.* ESV

Ezra 8:21 *Then I proclaimed a fast there, at the river, that we might humble ourselves before our God . . .* ESV

Luke 2:37 *. . . and then as a widow until she was eighty-four. She did not depart from the temple, worshiping with fasting and prayer night and day.* ESV

Zechariah 7:5 *Say to all the people of the land and the priests, When you fasted and mourned in the fifth month and in the seventh, for these seventy years, was it for me that you fasted?* ESV

Question 1: How would you generalize the purpose of the fasts above?

PURPOSE: Fasting for specific spiritual reasons.

In the previous Scriptures, the reasons for fasting generally focused on elevating God's presence in the lives of His people. With the exception of the Day of Atonement (which was prescribed by the Law), most Old Testament periods of fasting were called or undertaken for a specific spiritual reason. For example:

Isaiah 58:6-7 *Is not this the fast that I choose: to loose the bonds of wickedness, to undo the straps of the yoke, to let the oppressed go free, and to break every yoke? 7 Is it not to share your bread with the hungry and bring the homeless poor into your house; when you see the naked, to cover him, and not to hide yourself from your own flesh?* ESV

Question 2: What seven reasons for fasting are given in Isaiah 58:6-7?

1.

2.

3.

4.

5.

6.

7.

Question 3: Given the reasons for fasting in Isaiah's day, which ones might be reasons for fasting today?

Question 4: When you read these verses in Isaiah, what Scripture in Matthew comes to mind?

Question 5: In the following, record the purpose or reason for the fast.

Deuteronomy 9:18 *Then I lay prostrate before the Lord as before, forty days and forty nights. I neither ate bread nor drank water, because of all the sin that you had committed, in doing what was evil in the sight of the Lord to provoke him to anger.* ESV

1 Samuel 7:6 *So they gathered at Mizpah and drew water and poured it out before the Lord and fasted on that day and said there, "We have sinned against the Lord." And Samuel judged the people of Israel at Mizpah.* ESV

Nehemiah 9:1-2 . . . *the people of Israel were assembled with fasting and in sackcloth, . . . 2 And the Israelites separated themselves from all foreigners and stood and confessed their sins and the iniquities of their fathers.* ESV

Acts 13:2-3 *While they were worshiping the Lord and fasting, the Holy Spirit said, "Set apart for me Barnabas and Saul for the work to which I have called them." 3 Then after fasting and praying they laid their hands on them and sent them off.* ESV

2 Chronicles 20:3-4 *Then Jehoshaphat was afraid and set his face to seek the Lord, and proclaimed a fast throughout all Judah. 4 And Judah assembled to seek help from the Lord; from all the cities of Judah they came to seek the Lord.* ESV

1 Corinthians 7:5 *Do not deprive one another, except perhaps by agreement for a limited time, that you may devote yourselves to prayer; but then come together again, so that Satan may not tempt you because of your lack of self-control.* ESV

Daniel 9:3, 22-23 *Then I turned my face to the Lord God, seeking him by prayer and pleas for mercy with fasting and sackcloth and ashes. . . . 22 He made me understand, speaking with me and saying, "O Daniel, I have now come out to give you insight and understanding. 23 At the beginning of your pleas for mercy a word went out, and I have come to tell it to you, for you are greatly loved. Therefore consider the word and understand the vision."* ESV

SERIOUS FASTING

In order to discover the reason for fasting in the following passages, we would need to understand the context, which would require reading more than just a few verses. We've therefore provided the answers in the headings. These fasting events are all in response to some major crisis (personal, church, nation).

Genocide of the Jews

Esther 4:15-16 *Then Esther told them to reply to Mordecai, 16 "Go, gather all the Jews to be found in Susa, and hold a fast on my behalf, and do not eat or drink for three days, night or day. I and my young women will also fast as you do. Then I will go to the king, though it is against the law, and if I perish, I perish."* ESV

Judgment of God

Joel 1:14 *Consecrate a fast; call a solemn assembly. Gather the elders and all the inhabitants of the land to the house of the Lord your God, and cry out to the Lord.* ESV

Joel 2:12 *"Yet even now," declares the Lord, "return to me with all your heart, with fasting, with weeping, and with mourning.* ESV
[See also Jonah 3:6-8; 1 Kings 21:27; and 2 Samuel 12:16]

Destruction of temple and Jerusalem

Nehemiah 1:3-4 *And they said to me, "The remnant there in the province who had survived the exile is in great trouble and shame. The wall of Jerusalem is broken down, and its gates are destroyed by fire." 4 As soon as I heard these words I sat down and wept and mourned for days, and I continued fasting and praying before the God of heaven.* ESV

War

2 Samuel 1:12 *And they mourned and wept and fasted until evening for Saul and for Jonathan his son and for the people of the Lord and for the house of Israel, because they had fallen by the sword.* ESV
[See also 2 Chronicles 20:2-3 and Judges 20:25-26]

Return from exile

Ezra 8:21 *Then I proclaimed a fast there, at the river Ahava, that we might humble ourselves before our God, to seek from him a safe journey for ourselves, our children, and all our goods.* ESV

Illness

Psalms 35:13 *But I, when they were sick—I wore sackcloth; I afflicted myself with fasting; I prayed with head bowed on my chest.* ESV

DISCUSSION QUESTIONS

Question 6: What do you conclude is an appropriate reason to fast? What might be inappropriate?

Question 7: Do the reasons or purposes for the fasting and prayer outlined above apply today? Can you think of any examples?

CONCLUSION

Our purpose in Lessons 8 and 9 has been to introduce you to what the Bible says about fasting. Our hope is that you have a clearer understanding of fasting and the reasons it was employed. We encourage you to consider fasting in your life as God leads you in that direction. Fasting gives you no leverage with God, but it does change your perceptions and should enhance your prayer life. Use fasting as a tool to come closer to God.

For an excellent book on this subject, we recommend *A Hunger for God* by John Piper.

BONUS: Guidelines for fasting from food

1. Don't fast if you are sick or have health issues. Check with your doctor.

2. Don't fast if you need an immediate answer to a question or concern. Fasting is not likely to produce answers to time-critical questions.

3. Be led by God into fasting. Be sure your motives are right.

4. Always drink adequate amounts of water.

5. Start slowly. Don't begin with a 7-day fast. Start with one meal or one day. Extend your fasts as you desire once you are comfortable with the process. Educate yourself on fasting before you begin.

6. If you decide to fast regularly, make sure you have adequate recovery time. Your body will need time to adjust to a new routine.

7. An ideal way to begin a 24-hour fast is to begin after your evening meal. Thus, you will only miss breakfast and lunch.

8. Recover slowly. Don't eat a big meal after a fast. The longer the fasting period, the more slowly you should ease back to your normal routine.

What I Want to Remember

Enter some notes and information that you want to remember about this lesson. It might be a Scripture verse or two, something new you learned, something you want to do, something you want to change, or just something you want to be sure to remember.

Wisdom to Action
Challenge

How can you prepare your heart and mind for a meaningful fast? What sin do you need to confess, and what specific spiritual need will you intercede for during your next fast?

LESSON 10
How to Solve Problems Through Prayer

"When prayer fails, the world prevails, when prayer fails
the church loses its divine characteristics, its divine power;
the church is swallowed up by a proud ecclesiasticism,
and the world scoffs at its obvious impotence."
E. M. Bounds[8]

2 Chronicles 19:3-4, 7, 9, 11
*Nevertheless, some good is found in you, for you destroyed the
Asherahs out of the land, and have set your heart to seek God." 4
Jehoshaphat lived at Jerusalem. And he went out again among the
people, from Beersheba to the hill country of Ephraim, and brought
them back to the Lord, the God of their fathers. . . . 7 Now then, let the
fear of the Lord be upon you. Be careful what you do, for there is no
injustice with the Lord our God, or partiality or taking bribes.". . . 9
And he charged them: "Thus you shall do in the fear of the Lord, in
faithfulness, and with your whole heart: . . . 11 And behold, Amariah
the chief priest is over you in all matters of the Lord; and Zebadiah the
son of Ishmael, the governor of the house of Judah, in all the king's
matters, and the Levites will serve you as officers. Deal courageously,
and may the Lord be with the upright!" ESV*

2 Chronicles 20:1-6 [Jehoshaphat's Prayer]
*After this the Moabites and Ammonites, and with them some of the
Meunites, came against Jehoshaphat for battle. 2 Some men came and
told Jehoshaphat, "A great multitude is coming against you from
Edom, from beyond the sea; and, behold, they are in Hazazon-tamar"
(that is, Engedi). 3 Then Jehoshaphat was afraid and set his face to
seek the Lord, and proclaimed a fast throughout all Judah. 4 And Judah*

assembled to seek help from the Lord; from all the cities of Judah they came to seek the Lord.

5 And Jehoshaphat stood in the assembly of Judah and Jerusalem, in the house of the Lord, before the new court, 6 and said, "O Lord, God of our fathers, are you not God in heaven? You rule over all the kingdoms of the nations. In your hand are power and might, so that none is able to withstand you. ESV

As Jehoshaphat began to pray in 20:6 above, he proclaimed that God is interested in the problems of His people. He confirmed that God <u>rules</u> from heaven and He has the power and might to carry out His plans for His people. In fact, God has demonstrated that desire and capability all throughout history. Note what David said in the Psalms:

- Ps 55:22: Cast your burdens on the Lord.
- Ps 56:9: God is for him.
- Ps 68:19: God daily bears our burdens.

In the New Testament The Lord's Prayer confirms a personal and intimate desire for the people to call on the Lord for their needs. (Mt 6:5-13 and Luke 11:1-5)

Question 1: Look up what Jesus tells us to pray for in the following?

Mt 6:10

Mt 6:12

Mt 6:13

God is greater than our problems. He is the Creator, Healer, Savior, and Almighty God. He can speak anything into existence. He can deliver the incarnation of His Son

Jesus into the world. He can raise the dead. If you have doubts about what God can do, then you don't know God! But because He is sovereign, He decides what is needed and what He wants to accomplish. That's why He says He will answer when we pray according to His will.

Question 2: What should be our first response when we have needs?

Question 3: How would you personally describe or define what you think it means to seek the Lord?

Question 4: What can you identify in the 2 Chronicles passages above that would suggest it's just not about us personally?

This would suggest that your greatest asset may be the people that will pray for you!

God will give us a solution to our problems; we just have to persevere in prayer long enough to know, understand, and recognize His solution. We often stop praying long before God provides a solution. Or we don't recognize the solution because it is not what we asked for. We need to understand that the answer may be, wait! The people we are praying for may not be ready for God's solution. He may want other people to be part of the solution and those people or the logistics are not yet in place.

Therefore God's solutions might mean waiting (being patient) or receiving an answer that was not wanted or not expected.

Question 5: What does 2 Chron 20:6-12 have to say about the nature of our prayers?

Question 6: What does Ephesians Chapter 6 have to say about this subject?

Question 7: Can you identify a faith requirement in the 2 Chronicles passages (19:7 and 19:9)?

19:7

19:9

God's solutions are always the best!

Question 8: What is God's solution in 2 Chronicles 20:24?

CHALLENGE: What is the biggest problem in your life?

What I Want to Remember

Enter some notes and information that you want to remember about this lesson. It might be a Scripture verse or two, something new you learned, something you want to do, something you want to change, or just something you want to be sure to remember.

Wisdom to Action
Challenge

What seemingly insurmountable obstacle are you facing right now? How can you apply persistent, faith-filled prayer to this situation, trusting in God's transformative power?

APPENDIX A
Jesus' Prayer – John 17

Most scholars outline this chapter based on the three different groups of people Jesus prayed for:

17:1-5	Himself
17:6-19	Existing disciples
17:20-23	Future disciples (the church)

Jesus prayed the following for each group:

Himself:

17:1	to be glorified
17:2-4	His mission
17:5	reinstatement of previous glorified state

Existing Disciples:

17:6-10	their status and situation
17:11-16	they would be preserved and protected
17:17-19	that they would be sanctified

Future Disciples:

17:21-22	unity
17:20-23	that the world would know God sent Jesus

Five themes can be easily identified:

1. Giving:
The theme of what God gives Jesus or believers and what Jesus gives His followers is spread throughout the chapter:

17:2	eternal life
17:4	work
17:8, 14	His words
17:11-12	name

17:13	His joy
17:5, 22, 24	His glory
17:26	love

2. Unity:

The three kinds of unity are described in the prayer:

17:1-6, 7, 21	Christ in unity with the Father
17:10, 21, 23	Believers in unity with Christ and God
17:11, 21, 23	Believers in unity with other believers

3. Glory:

The word "glory" occurs seven times with various meanings in the chapter. The primary implication is that Jesus will reveal the source of that glory. Ps 86:9-12 tells us about glorifying God:

(a) to praise His name, and
(b) to honor His commandments

4. Disciple:

In verses 17:6-8, Jesus outlines what it means to be a disciple:

17:6	to understand we were chosen by God
17:6	to obey God's commands and decrees
17:7-8	to believe and know Jesus came from God
17:10	to bring glory to Jesus

5. World:

Jesus gave His disciples instructions regarding the world in John 17:14-23:

- They should live in the world, not withdraw from it.
- They should demonstrate their faith to the world.
- They should face the troubles of the world.
- They should make it known that Jesus was sent by God.

Jesus knew that remaining in the world would be challenging and dangerous for the disciples. They would need the power of His name for protection. Hostility toward Jesus and God would fall on the heads of the disciples. But Jesus called down the power of God's name so that they could be one in will and purpose.

PRAYING JOHN 17

John 17:1-5
I pray that I will know, exalt, and honor Christ so that He is glorified through me by the successful completion of the work He gives me to do.

John 17:6-19
I pray that I will believe, accept, and obey the Word of Truth so that I might (1) reveal it to my friends and others that I meet, (2) be protected from the evil one by the power of His Name, (3) be one with Christ as He is one with God the Father, (4) have the joy of Christ in me; and (5) be truly sanctified.

John 17:20-26
I pray that I will be one with other believers and one with Christ in order that I might proclaim the Gospel and the love of God through word and deed, all to the glory of God.

APPENDIX B
The Lord's Prayer

Our Father, in Heaven.
Recognizing God as "Father" implies that we are His children, part of the family of God. He is the creator and sustainer of life and He cares like a parent.

Hallowed be Your name.
"Hallowed" means holy. We must acknowledge and give honor and praise to God. God's honor should be a top priority, and our lives should honor and proclaim His Name.

Your kingdom come, Your will be done.
We acknowledge God as ruler of the world. He is our King and Sovereign Lord. We must choose to obey His will. Our lives should reflect His plan. He should be the priority in our lives and His commandments should rule our lifestyle.

Give us each day our daily bread.
TODAY: Our God is in control. He is sovereign and will provide for all our needs. God provides and I accept what He gives, regardless of the size or type of His daily provision. I put my future and well-being in His hands.

Forgive our sins, as we forgive those who sin against us.
YESTERDAY: We examine our relationships and repair those that need to be fixed. Jesus forgives us so we understand the desire to forgive others. But our forgiveness for sin comes only from the grace of God and the shed blood of Christ. We do not take revenge or hold grudges against others.

And lead us not into temptation, but deliver us from evil.
TOMORROW: We pray to God for His future protection
and deliverance. He will walk through every valley with us
and hold our hand when necessary. Our struggle is with
the dark powers of evil and spiritual forces in the heavenly
realms. We need the power of God to protect us from
Satan. Thus, we put on the full armor of God.

For Yours is the kingdom, power, and glory forever.
The prayer ends with praise and a focus on God,

Amen!
The word "Amen," means "So be it."[9]

APPENDIX C
Simple Facts About Prayer

- Prayer is simply talking with God.
- We can pray about anything, any time, any place.
- God does hear our prayers.
- God answers one of three ways: Yes, No, Wait (Maybe?).
- Four Types of Prayer: Adoration, Confession, Thanksgiving, and Supplication. (A.C. T. S.)
- God will hear regardless of our physical position.
- Faith is vital in prayer.
- We can't expect God to grant our requests if we are unwilling to grant His (obedience).
- We must deal with known sin, before we can expect God to act on our prayers.
- Prayer is hard work, thus, patience and perseverance are needed.
- We must approach God in humility.
- We can be bold and confident, because He fully loves and accepts us.
- When we pray aloud, concentrate on talking to God, not on impressing others.
- We must use our brain when we pray. Don't just repeat phrases.
- Pray expectantly. We must be specific in our requests.
- Wait expectantly. Take time to listen.

APPENDIX D
Prayer for the Heart

I pray also that the eyes of your *heart* may be enlightened
in order that you may know the hope to which he has called you,
the riches of his glorious inheritance in the saints,
and his incomparably great power for us who believe.
Eph 1:18-19 NIV

HEART — What Does Scripture Say?

God knows the heart of each person (1 Sam. 16:7). Since a
person speaks and acts from his heart, he is to guard it
well (Prov. 4:23; Matt. 15:18-19). The most important duty
of man is to love God with the whole heart (Matt. 22:37).
With the heart man believes in Christ and so experiences
both love from God and the presence of Christ in his heart
(Rom. 5:5; 10:9-10; Eph. 3:17).

In the Bible the word *heart* has a much broader meaning
than it does to the modern mind today. The heart
represents that which is <u>central to man</u>. Nearly all the
references to the heart in the Bible refer to some aspect of
human personality. For example:

All *emotions* are experienced by the heart:

Love and hate	(Ps 105:25; 1 Pet 1:22)
Joy and sorrow	(Eccl 2:10; John 16:6)
Peace and bitterness	(Ezek 27:31; Col 3:15)
Courage and fear	(Gen 42:28; Amos 2:16)

The thinking processes of man are said to be carried out by
the heart. This intellectual activity corresponds to what
would be called the <u>mind</u> in English. Thus, the heart may:

think	(Esth 6:6)
understand	(Job 38:36)
imagine	(Jer 9:14)
remember	(Deut 4:9)
be wise	(Prov 2:10)
speak to itself	(Deut 7:17)
have purpose	(Acts 11:23)
have intention	(Heb 4:12)
have will	(Eph 6:6)

The heart often represents someone's true character or personality:

purity or evil	(Jer 3:17; Matt 5:8)
sincerity or hardness	(Ex 4:21; Col 3:22)
maturity or rebelliousness	(Ps 101:2; Jer 5:23

Paul Speaks of the Heart?

1Thes 3:13 *May he strengthen your **hearts** so that you will be blameless and holy in the presence of our God and Father when our Lord Jesus comes with all his holy ones.* (NIV)

2 Thes 2:16-17 *May our Lord Jesus Christ himself and God our Father, who loved us and by his grace gave us eternal encouragement and good hope, encourage your **hearts** and strengthen you in every good deed and word.* (NIV)

2 Thes 3:5 *May the Lord direct your **hearts** into God's love and Christ's perseverance.* (NIV)

Why Pray For the Heart

Prov 6:16-18 *There are six things the LORD hates, seven that are detestable to him. . . a **heart** that devises wicked schemes, feet that are quick to rush into evil,*

Prov 11:20 *The LORD detests men of **perverse heart** . . .*

Gen 6:5 *The LORD saw how great man's wickedness on the earth had become, and that every inclination of the thoughts of his **heart** was only evil all the time.*

Jer 17:5 *This is what the LORD says: "Cursed is the one who trusts in man, who depends on flesh for his strength and whose **heart** turns away from the LORD."*

Matt 12:34 *You brood of vipers, how can you who are evil say anything good? For out of the overflow of the **heart** the mouth speaks.*

Ps 101:4 *Men of **perverse heart** shall be far from me; I will have nothing to do with evil.*

Heb 3:10 *That is why I was angry with that generation, and I said, 'Their **hearts** are always going astray, and they have not known my ways.'*

Eph 4:18 *They are darkened in their understanding and separated from the life of God because of the ignorance that is in them due to the **hardening of their hearts**.*

Prov 12:23 *A prudent man keeps his knowledge to himself, but the **heart of fools** blurts out folly.*

APPENDIX E
Answered Prayer in Scripture
(15 Examples)

Hannah Prays for a Son (1 Samuel 1): Deeply sorrowful due to her barrenness, Hannah earnestly prayed for a son. God answered her plea, and she gave birth to the prophet Samuel.

Hezekiah's Prayer for Healing (2 Kings 20): King Hezekiah, struck with a fatal illness, wept and prayed to God for healing. God heard him and extended his life by fifteen years.

Elijah Prays for Fire (1 Kings 18): In a contest of faith against the prophets of Baal, Elijah boldly prayed for fire from heaven. God dramatically consumed the sacrifice, demonstrating His power in answering Elijah's prayer.

Daniel's Prayer in the Lion's Den (Daniel 6): Despite a decree forbidding prayer to anyone but the king, Daniel continued his prayer life. He was thrown into a lion's den, but God miraculously protected him and his faith was rewarded.

Nehemiah Prays to Rebuild Jerusalem (Nehemiah 1-2): Nehemiah mourned for the ruined state of Jerusalem. He prayed for favor with the king, and God granted his wish, opening a path for him to rebuild the city's walls.

The Church Prays for Peter's Release (Acts 12): When Peter was imprisoned, the church gathered in prayer. An angel of the Lord appeared, Peter's chains fell off, and he was led out of prison.

Jesus' Prayer Before the Transfiguration (Luke 9): Jesus' prayer on the mountain led to a dazzling display of His glory, where Moses and Elijah appeared alongside Him.

Jesus Prays in Gethsemane (Matthew 26): Jesus, in deep agony before His crucifixion, prayed for strength and submission to God's will. His prayer gave Him the courage to face the trial before Him.

The Thief on the Cross (Luke 23): As Jesus was crucified, one of the criminals beside Him recognized His innocence and asked to be remembered. Jesus promised him paradise, granting salvation in response to a moment of sincere prayer.

Paul and Silas Pray in Prison (Acts 16): Imprisoned for their faith, Paul and Silas chose to pray and sing hymns to God. An earthquake shook the prison, their bonds were loosed, and they witnessed to the jailer, leading to his salvation.

Moses Parting the Red Sea (Exodus 14): Faced by the pursuing Egyptian army and the Red Sea blocking their escape, the Israelites cried out to God. Moses stretched out his staff, and God miraculously parted the waters, allowing the Israelites to cross safely.

David's Plea for Deliverance from Saul (1 Samuel 17-18): Persecuted by King Saul, David prayed for God's protection and guidance. God empowered David to defeat the mighty warrior Goliath and eventually David became king himself.

Elijah's Prayer for Rain (1 Kings 18): After a prolonged drought, Elijah prayed for rain. God answered his prayer, sending a great downpour that ended the famine in the land.

The Centurion's Servant Healed (Matthew 8:5-13): A Roman centurion approached Jesus, pleading for his servant's healing. Recognizing Jesus' authority, the centurion expressed faith that Jesus could heal his servant from a distance. Jesus commended the centurion's faith and granted his request, healing the servant at that very moment.

The Blind Man Bartimaeus (Mark 10): Begging by the roadside, blind Bartimaeus called out to Jesus in faith and prayer. Jesus heard him, healed his blindness, and restored his sight.

APPENDIX F
Paul's Prayers (NIV)

Eph 1:15-23
For this reason, ever since I heard about your faith in the Lord Jesus and your love for all the saints, I have not stopped giving thanks for you, remembering you in my prayers. I keep asking that the God of our Lord Jesus Christ, the glorious Father, may give you the Spirit of wisdom and revelation, so that you may know him better. I pray also that the eyes of your heart may be enlightened in order that you may know the hope to which he has called you, the riches of his glorious inheritance in the saints, and his incomparably great power for us who believe. That power is like the working of his mighty strength, which he exerted in Christ when he raised him from the dead and seated him at his right hand in the heavenly realms, far above all rule and authority, power and dominion, and every title that can be given, not only in the present age but also in the one to come. And God placed all things under his feet and appointed him to be head over everything for the church, which is his body, the fullness of him who fills everything in every way.

Eph 3:16-21
I pray that out of his glorious riches he may strengthen you with power through his Spirit in your inner being, so that Christ may dwell in your hearts through faith. And I pray that you, being rooted and established in love, may have power, together with all the saints, to grasp how wide and long and high and deep is the love of Christ, and to know this love that surpasses knowledge – that you may be filled to the measure of all the fullness of God. Now to him who is able to do immeasurably more than all we ask or imagine, according to his power that is at work within us, to him be glory in the church and in Christ Jesus throughout all generations, for ever and ever! Amen.

Eph 6:18-20
Pray in the Spirit on all occasions with all kinds of prayers and requests. With this in mind, be alert and always keep on praying for all the saints. Pray also for me, that whenever I open my mouth, words may be given me so that I will fearlessly make known the mystery of the gospel, for which I am an ambassador in chains. Pray that I may declare it fearlessly, as I should.

Phil 1:3-6
I thank my God every time I remember you. In all my prayers for all of you, I always pray with joy because of your partnership in the gospel from the first day until now, being confident of this, that he who began a good work in you will carry it on to completion until the day of Christ Jesus.

Phil 1:9-11
And this is my prayer: that your love may abound more and more in knowledge and depth of insight, so that you may be able to discern what is best and may be pure and blameless until the day of Christ, filled with the fruit of righteousness that comes through Jesus Christ — to the glory and praise of God.

1 Thes 1:2-3
We always thank God for all of you, mentioning you in our prayers. We continually remember before our God and Father your work produced by faith, your labor prompted by love, and your endurance inspired by hope in our Lord Jesus Christ.

1 Tim 2:1-2
I urge, then, first of all, that requests, prayers, intercession and thanksgiving be made for everyone – for kings and all those in authority, that we may live peaceful and quiet lives in all godliness and holiness.

2 Tim 1:3-4
I thank God, whom I serve, as my forefathers did, with a clear conscience, as night and day I constantly remember you in my prayers. Recalling your tears, I long to see you, so that I may be filled with joy.

1 Cor 1:4-9
I always thank God for you because of his grace given you in Christ Jesus. For in him you have been enriched in every way – in all your speaking and in all your knowledge – because our testimony about Christ was confirmed in you. Therefore you do not lack any spiritual gift as you eagerly wait for our Lord Jesus Christ to be revealed. He will keep you strong to the end, so that you will be blameless on the day of our Lord Jesus Christ. God, who has called you into fellowship with his Son Jesus Christ our Lord, is faithful.

2 Cor 13:7, 9

Now we pray to God that you will not do anything wrong. Not that people will see that we have stood the test but that you will do what is right even though we may seem to have failed. We are glad whenever we are weak but you are strong; and our prayer is for your perfection.

Col 1:3-6

We always thank God, the Father of our Lord Jesus Christ, when we pray for you, because we have heard of your faith in Christ Jesus and of the love you have for all the saints – the faith and love that spring from the hope that is stored up for you in heaven and that you have already heard about in the word of truth, the gospel that has come to you.

Col 1:9-14

For this reason, since the day we heard about you, we have not stopped praying for you and asking God to fill you with the knowledge of his will through all spiritual wisdom and understanding. And we pray this in order that you may live a life worthy of the Lord and may please him in every way: bearing fruit in every good work, growing in the knowledge of God, being strengthened with all power according to his glorious might so that you may have great endurance and patience, and joyfully giving thanks to the Father, who has qualified you to share in the inheritance of the saints in the kingdom of light. For he has rescued us from the dominion of darkness and brought us into the kingdom of the Son he loves, in whom we have redemption, the forgiveness of sins.

Col 2:1-3

I want you to know how much I am struggling for you and for those at Laodicea, and for all who have not met me personally. My purpose is that they may be encouraged in heart and united in love, so that they may have the full riches of complete understanding, in order that they may know the mystery of God, namely, Christ, in whom are hidden all the treasures of wisdom and knowledge.

Col 4:2-6, 12

Devote yourselves to prayer, being watchful and thankful. And pray for us, too, that God may open a door for our message, so that we may proclaim the mystery of Christ, for which I am in chains. Pray that I may proclaim it clearly, as I should. Be wise in the way you act toward outsiders; make the most of every opportunity. Let your conversation be always full of grace, seasoned with salt, so that you may know how to answer everyone. Epaphras, who is one of you and a servant of Christ Jesus, sends greetings. He is always wrestling in prayer for you, that you may stand firm in all the will of God, mature and fully assured.

1 Thes 3:10-13

Night and day we pray most earnestly that we may see you again and supply what is lacking in your faith. Now may our God and Father himself and our Lord Jesus clear the way for us to come to you. May the Lord make your love increase and overflow for each other and for everyone else, just as ours does for you. May he strengthen your hearts so that you will be blameless and holy in the presence of our God and Father when our Lord Jesus comes with all his holy ones.

1 Thes 5:16-18

Be joyful always; pray continually; give thanks in all circumstances, for this is God's will for you in Christ Jesus.

2 Thes 1:11-12

With this in mind, we constantly pray for you, that our God may count you worthy of his calling, and that by his power he may fulfill every good purpose of yours and every act prompted by your faith. We pray this so that the name of our Lord Jesus may be glorified in you, and you in him, according to the grace of our God and the Lord Jesus Christ.

2 Thes 3:1-2

Finally, brothers, pray for us that the message of the Lord may spread rapidly and be honored, just as it was with you. And pray that we may be delivered from wicked and evil men, for not everyone has faith.

Transformation Road Map

Primary Takeaways

1: Prayer is an essential tool for deepening one's relationship with God and accessing His power, wisdom, and peace. Regular and earnest prayer will delight the heart of God.

2: Effective prayer requires aligning oneself with God's will and character. This alignment requires living in accordance to God's commands and maintaining a close, abiding relationship with Jesus.

3: Prayer must be rooted in humility, praise, and confidence in God's character and promises. This involves waiting on Him with patience and trust, seeking righteousness, and pursuing goals aligned with His will.

4: Sin and a lack of genuine devotion, whether through hypocrisy, pride, or unresolved conflict, create significant barriers that hinder God's response to our prayers. We must actively examine our hearts, confess and repent of sin, and prioritize obedience, in order to maintain an open channel of communication with God.

5: Prayer should be a constant and intimate communion with God. We should intercede specifically for the salvation of the lost and for the spiritual growth and well-being of fellow believers.

6: Our prayer should be fueled by a desire for His will to be done and His glory to be revealed in all aspects of life. God desires that we diligently seek Him in prayer.

7: Prayer can cultivate a heart of humility and righteousness, increasing inner strength and a peace that surpasses all understanding, producing a deeper and more intimate relationship with Him.

8: We can approach God with boldness, humbly seeking His blessings, protection, and empowerment. Our lives should be characterized by the boldness of prayer which is rooted in a desire to honor God and serve others.

9: Fasting, when coupled with prayer, intensifies our focus on God, deepens our humility, and amplifies our spiritual power. Fasting can be a valuable discipline for seeking God's presence, confessing sin, and interceding for specific needs. It can empower our prayers with increased urgency and effectiveness in addressing specific spiritual needs or crises.

10: Prayer can tap into God's power and wisdom, enabling us to overcome any obstacle and find solutions aligned with His perfect will. Persistent prayer unlocks His transformative power in our lives and circumstances.

What are you being called to pray about?

Leader Guide

This Guide is designed to give a group leader answers and additional information to effectively lead a discussion of each lesson in this book.

Tips For Leading

We recommend that you begin a group discussion by reading an appropriate Scripture. It may be one that you will cover in the material or another related passage you have chosen. This will do several things:

- Allow time for everyone to get settled.
- Remind everyone of the subject and bring their minds to a common focus.
- Provide a transition from the previous activity.

Additional ice-breakers are usually not necessary, but if your group is new or members don't know each other well, you could have someone give their testimony/story at the beginning of each week. If you sense that the group needs additional focus before you begin with the discussion, conduct a short discussion about the themes of the lesson or ask about the meaning of a particular term associated with the lesson.

Goals

The discussion should center around the questions in the lesson. But remember that each person in your group has different goals and is at a different place in his or her Christian walk. Jesus may be an old friend to some but a new acquaintance to others. The dynamic of the group will vary depending on the nature of the participants.

Your goal as the Leader should be to foster understanding and familiarity with Scripture. For new believers or participants who are not comfortable with the Bible, your goal should be to help them get over that hurdle and begin to seek knowledge and understanding from His Word.

More mature participants will probably dig deeper to find personal meaning and understanding. They may particularly desire to discuss application questions and issues.

Prayer

Unless you have an outstanding person of prayer in your group, you as the leader should wrap up your discussion time with prayer that specifically reflects the discussion and the themes, purpose, and focus of the lesson.

Answers

LESSON 1 What Conditions are Necessary for Answered Prayer?
Question 1
"faith in God" and "do not doubt" in your heart)
"believe what he says" (know you will receive it)
Question 2
It is both. If it is not both there is contradiction and doubt.
Question 3
The reference here is to Abraham's complete confidence in God – true faith. Abraham did not waver – he was fully persuaded. If we doubt that God will or can do it, then faith is compromised.
Question 4
Faith comes from hearing the message, and the message is heard through the word of Christ (Christ's teachings, etc)
Question 5
If you are just hoping, then you do not have adequate faith. You may have doubts and are not fully persuaded. There is a big difference in I know He will answer vs. I hope He will answer.
Question 6
Obedience; submission; yielding to His will.
LEADER: We suggest discussing participant answers in some depth.
Question 7
It is consistent with what God wants to do or wants to happen. For example we know that God wants all to be saved ("none should perish"), therefore, He would respond positively to a request for salvation. In general, it can be said that God desires obedience, seeking Him with all our heart, being transformed, and becoming sanctified by the Holy Spirit
Question 8
John 6:38-39
Jesus says He will lose none of those given to Him by the Father (salvation).
LEADER: You might ask, "Does the reference to last day imply answers might be delayed until Jesus return?"
Romans 12:2
We are to learn to perceive and discern "the will of God" while we are being transformed. God will not answer in a way that is in conflict with His will.

Ephesians 1:11
For those that have believed on the Lord Jesus, and confessed Him as Lord, they will receive an inheritance of eternal life in the presence of God. And, although difficult for some to understand, we who have believed and were chosen by God (predestined): we are the "Elect."

1 Thessalonians 4:3
We are to be set apart (holy); we have a holy purpose; we are being purified in the sanctification process.

1 Thessalonians 4:4-8 *that each one of you know how to control his own body in holiness and honor, 5 not in the passion of lust like the Gentiles who do not know God; 6 that no one transgress and wrong his brother in this matter, because the Lord is an avenger in all these things, as we told you beforehand and solemnly warned you. 7 For God has not called us for impurity, but in holiness. 8 Therefore whoever disregards this, disregards not man but God, who gives his Holy Spirit to you.* ESV

Question 9
It's God's will that we be molded and conformed to the image of Christ. We are to imitate Christ. Thus, we must seek after Him and be in lock step with His ways. When we do that we will ultimately be one with Him and our desires will be the same as His. We are being transformed! But the road may be bumpy.

Question 10
       a. Keep His commandments.
       b. Do what pleases Him.

Question 11
       a. We believe in the name of His Son Jesus.
       b. We love one another.

Question 12
Proverbs 15:8 *The sacrifice of the wicked is an abomination to the Lord, but the prayer of the **upright** is acceptable to him.* ESV The prayer of the upright (righteous) **pleases Him.**

Hebrews 11:6 *And without **faith** it is impossible to please him, for whoever would draw near to God must **believe that he exists** and that he rewards those who seek him.* ESV Without faith it is impossible to **please Him.**

Question 13
Upright means righteous; strong moral character; ethical; honorable; honest and trustworthy.
LEADER: You might ask," Will prayer be answered for a Christian who is generally good, but does not attend church?"

Question 14
Ask in my name

Question 15
"Name" has a much broader meaning: They believed there was a vital connection between the name and the person it identified. A name somehow represented the nature of the person. Jesus taught His disciples to pray, "Hallowed be Your name" (Matt 6:9). Christians were described by the apostle Paul as those who "name the name of the Lord" (2 Tim 2:19). A true understanding of the exalted Jesus is often connected with a statement about His name. Thus, Jesus "has by inheritance obtained a more excellent name" than the angels (Heb 1:4). According to Paul, "God also has highly exalted Him

and given Him the name which is above every name" (Phil 2:9).
"(from Nelson's Illustrated Bible Dictionary,)
Thus, power and authority were associated with claiming a "name" This implied connection and agreement. Phil 2:9-11 says that His Name is above every Name!
Meanings: (1) We are in thorough accord; (2) it implies His whole divine nature; (3) it is the entire administration of God; or (4) His power and presence.

Question 16
Jesus, His Name, and His divine nature deserve and are worthy of worship, by everyone, not just His followers. This includes everyone alive and all those who have died, implying the spirit/soul is eternal.

Question 17
(a) We abide (remain) in Jesus,
(b) His words abide (remain) in us.

Question 18
Short Answer: (a) union and fellowship with Jesus, (b) God in form of Holy Spirit indwelling us, (c) mutually indwelling, (d) completeness.
Long Answer: This is not an easy question to answer in a way that will produce deep meaning and understanding. Some might say it is the unbroken connection between God and His people. It might be described as fellowship between God and man. It is a relationship that is close, united, and intimate. And, the degree to which any one person abides will vary significantly – not everyone abides in the same way and to the same extent.
Wuest's Word Studies says that abiding in the New Testament means to maintain unbroken fellowship, to be constantly present to help, and to put forth constant influence upon someone. In the Gospel of John, God is said to abide or remain in Christ or to be continually operative in Him by His divine influence and energy (John 14:10).

> John 14:10   *Don't you believe that I am in the Father, and that the Father is in me? The words I say to you are not just my own. Rather, it is the Father, living in me, who is doing his work.* NIV

Jesus wants us to be "with Him" (Mk 3:14). Time spent with Jesus by reading, studying, meditating, fasting, or praying to Him is not just a priority, it is *absolutely essential* in our Christian walk. This is necessary in order to develop a growing love relationship with God through Jesus. If this is not accomplished then our faith walk will lack focus, power, and support – nothing will work exactly right.

Question 19
Bear fruit.
In John 15:8 true disciples bear fruit, which means: God has appointed us to bear fruit that will abide, thus obeying the Great Commission. True believers are the only ones that can abide. The focus is on evangelism and the means is prayer.
This might also have reference to the fruit of the Spirit:
Galatians 5:22 *But the fruit of the Spirit is love, joy, peace, patience, kindness, goodness, faithfulness,* ESV

Question 20
Ephesians 4:12 Serving the Body: building up the body of Christ (bearing fruit).

Be bold and pray in the Spirit on all occasions.

Romans 12:7 Using our gifts in serving for the common good.
1 Peter 4:10 Serving one another (others)
Question 21
It's not just any service, but one that
will complete the Great Commission. Thus, the focus is on people –
winning converts. The reference may also be to the "fruit of the Spirit."
Question 22
    1. (a) Faith in God, (b) Believe you will receive
    2. Pray according to His will
    3. Obey His commands; do what pleases Him
    4. Ask in His Name
    5. (a) Remain(abide) in Christ (b) His words remain in us
    6. Bear fruit

DISCUSSION AND THOUGHT QUESTIONS
1. NO! God requires conformity and obedience to all conditions. Fellowship,
            relationship, and commitment are all requirements of
            knowing Christ. It's all or nothing.
2. Conformity to one almost assures conformity to all!
3. (1) trust and obey, (2) yield and surrender, (3) seek with all your heart (Jer
29:12-13), an d (4) a disciple
4. There are conditions placed on us if God is going to do what we ask.
Otherwise, God would be obligated in some way
to answer all our prayers. Fundamentally we are to call on Him
in truth, fear Him, and love Him.
Psalms 145:17-20 says, "*The Lord is righteous in all his ways and kind in all his
works. 18 The Lord is near to all who call on him, to all who call on him in
truth. 19 He fulfills the desire of those who fear him; he also hears their cry and
saves them. 20 The Lord preserves all who love him, but all the wicked he will
destroy.*" ESV
5. (1) He could, but there is no guarantee or actual promise to do so.
(2) Prayer for salvation: YES. (3) Otherwise: Probably NO
6. CHRIST 2 Corinthians 1:20 *For all the promises of God find their Yes in him.
That is why it is through him that we utter our Amen to God for his glory*. ESV

LESSON 2 How Can I Be Effective in Prayer?
Question 1
(1) Right standing with God, (2) purity of heart, and (3) doing the right thing.
Question 2
Steadfast = "devoted to the task of prayer" persistent.
Watchful = alert and expecting God's response.
Thanksgiving = expecting God's answer will be what you need. and being
grateful for however He answers your prayer.
Question 3
Heartily = wholeheartedly; thoroughly; with gusto; completely or entirely
1 Corinthians 15:58 *Therefore, my beloved brothers, be steadfast, immovable,
always abounding in the work of the Lord, knowing that in the Lord your labor
is not in vain.* ESV
Question 4
It is to be continuing, maybe until an answer is received. We are to keep on
asking, seeking and knocking. We are to persevere in prayer. Giving yourself

fully to pray means daily or regularly, seriously, being committed, and making it a priority.

Question 5

Luke 18:1 *And he told them a parable to the effect that they ought always to pray and not lose heart.* ESV

This verse describes prayer and then Jesus introduces a parable which was intended to teach us that we're to pray and not lose heart.

Important characteristics of praise

Psalm 29:2	Praise honors God the Father
Psalm 22:3	God inhabits the praise of His people
2 Chronicles 5:13	Praise sensitizes us to His presence
Acts 16:25-26	Praise breaks the enemy's oppression
Psalm 150:2	Praise confuses the forces of darkness

Psalm 119:164   Do it regularly

Question 6

Devoted; committed; waiting patiently; delight (worship and praise); standing firm; being in Christ (in the Spirit). The English for "waiting" then becomes to be united, mutually involved, interlaced, or woven together.

Question 7:

2 Kings 22:19 *because your <u>heart was penitent</u>, and you humbled yourself before the Lord, when you heard how I spoke against this place and against its inhabitants, that they should become a desolation and a curse, and you have <u>torn your clothes and wept before me</u>, I also have heard you, declares the Lord.* ESV

Proverbs 3:34 *Toward the scorners he is scornful, but <u>to the humble he gives favor.</u>* ESV

Luke 18:13-14 *But the tax collector, standing far off, <u>would not even lift up his eyes to heaven, but beat his breast</u>, saying, 'God, be merciful to me, a sinner!' 14 I tell you, this man went down to his house justified, rather than the other. For everyone who exalts himself will be humbled, but the <u>one who humbles himself will be exalted."</u>* ESV

Psalms 35:13 *But I, when they were sick—I <u>wore sackcloth</u>; I <u>afflicted myself with fasting;</u> I <u>prayed with head bowed</u> on my chest.* ESV

Question 8

James 4:10	Be exalted
2 Chron 7:14	Sin forgiven and land healed
2 Kings 22:20	Die in peace; not see the evil of "this place"
Pr 3:34	God will give grace
Lk 18:13-14	Be exalted

Question 9

Hear; Listen

Question 10.

a) Do not be quick with your words, guard your lips and wait to respond; do not be hasty, think about what you will say. Think before you speak.

Question 11.

Ans. b) Let your words be few! Don't ramble on. Be succinct.

Ans. Ecclesiastes 5:1-2 *Guard your steps when you go to the house of God. To draw near to listen is better than to offer the sacrifice of fools, for they do not know that they are doing evil. 2 Be not rash with your mouth, nor let your heart be hasty to utter a word before God, for God is in heaven and you are on*

earth. Therefore let your words be few. ESV
Question 12
Romans 4:21 *fully convinced that God was able*
to do what he had promised. ESV
I am fully persuaded that God will keep His promises.
I have no real doubt.
Question 13
(a) Salvation (generally)
(b) The following are all from Col 1:9-12
(c) Filled with the knowledge of His will
(d) To walk worthy of the LORD; fully pleasing to Him
(e) Bear fruit in all good works
(f) Increase in knowledge of God
(g) Strengthened with His power, endurance, patience, and joy
LEADER: Note that praying the type of prayers prayed by Paul are almost all consistent with the will of God. See Appendix F for a listing of Paul's prayers.
Question 14
1. upright; righteous
2. pray in the Spirit
3. be *devoted* to prayer
4. delight in the Lord
5. patience
6. praise
7. perseverance; persistence
8. humbly come to altar and ask
9. listen for and to the response
10. confidence

LESSON 3 What are the Hindrances to Answered Prayer?
Question 1a
2 Samuel 24:1 We can anger God and He will take action against us!
1 Chronicles 21:1 God will use both His own people (David above) and Satan to discipline His people.
Acts 17:28 He formed us, He is conforming us, and we are His
1 John 1:10 If we refuse to recognize and acknowledge our sin, then we are not children of God. True believers recognize their sins.
Question 1b
Isa 29:13   heart are far from Me
Mal 1:7-8   bringing polluted sacrifices
Mt 15:9   following the rules of men
Question 2
Thread: These verses are all about worship
Rules: Hypocritical worship; External rules that destroy the internal desire; traditions and practices that take precedence over God's laws, statues, ordinances (His will); Rigid worship routine; requirement to have certain spiritual gifts in order to speak or be member; legalism; no true love or worship.
Question 3
Proverbs 28:9 *If one turns away his ear from hearing the law, even his prayer is an abomination.* ESV

Don't give to church either tithe or offering. Don't' bear fruit; Don't use spiritual gifts; Don't serve.

Question 4

Pride: to be seen and heard by others – not to worship God or serve others.

Question 5

Want to exalt self; pride: look how important I am; church membership on resume; are involved in ministry for personal gain, not to serve others. Their talk is not consistent with their walk.

Question 6

Pride can impact praying, tithing, fasting, and serving. It can impact relationships with other believers. It can keep you away from church because you think you are better than others or don't need to spend time in worship with other believers.

Question 7

(1) let's make a deal, (2) personal gain, (3) force God to act on your behalf, (4) the longer we pray is more effective that short prayers of others, (5) if we say right thing the right way that will be magic button to God granting wishes, (6) self-indulgence (my pleasures), and (7) simply asking with the wrong motives.

Question 8:

(1) money for new car rather than transportation, (2) win the lottery, (3) win a game, (4) success in stock market, or (5) personal wants.

Question 9:

Disobedience; Rejecting God's Word or His teaching or commands.

Question 10

Glorify God, the Father

LEADER: You might ask: "Why do you think God desires glory?"

Question 11

The importance of family in God's plan is obvious in Scripture. Here we have the poor treatment of the spouse, disrespect for family, and dishonorable behavior. This disrespects the family and people who are made in the image of God.

Matthew 5:22-24 *But I say to you that everyone who is angry with his brother will be liable to judgment; whoever insults his brother will be liable to the council; and whoever says, 'You fool!' will be liable to the hell of fire. 23 So if you are offering your gift at the altar and there remember that your brother has something against you, 24 leave your gift there before the altar and go. First be reconciled to your brother, and then come and offer your gift.* ESV

Question 12

If you don't know what to pray, pray the Lord's Prayer.

Question 13

Work and family responsibilities; loud family environment. LEADER: We will discuss "location" at the end of Lesson 5

Question 14 n/a

Question 15 n/a

Question 16 n/a

Question 17 n/a

LESSON 4 Who and What Should I Pray For?

Question 1

We must believe *in the heart* that God raised Jesus from death
Why? Because it is with heart we believe and are justified

Question 2

a. Everyone (all people)
b. Kings (government leaders)
c. Those in high positions (those in authority)

Question 3

Bosses, parents, teachers, pastors, police, government, etc

Question 4

a. Live peaceful, quiet lives
b. In godliness and holiness
 c. To be saved
d. Come to know the truth

Question 5

(a) Understanding in order to govern.
(b) Ability to discern between good and evil.
God granted that wish and no other king would ever match Solomon's unique
wisdom and prosperity. But, in Eccl after searching for the secret to life and
happiness, he concluded that it simply came down to "fearing God and
keeping His commandments."

Question 6

1. Call on the elders to pray (leaders)
2. Anoint with oil
3. Pray in faith and confidence
4. Confess sin
5. Be righteous

Question 7

Yes, because the Jews are God's chosen
people and Israel His Promised Land. The Jews and Jerusalem have a
special place in the heart of God.

Question 8

We should pray for our own cities (See the prayer in Daniel 9)

Question 9

Believers (the Elect). **LEADER:** You might discuss the term "saints" and
what it means in both secular and Christian contexts.

Question 10

No. Don't neglect the church!
James 1:5-6 If any of you lacks wisdom, let him ask God, who gives
generously to all without reproach, and it will be given him. 6 But let
him ask in faith, with no doubting, for the one who doubts is like a
wave of the sea that is driven and tossed by the wind. ESV
James 5:13 13 Is anyone among you suffering? Let him pray. Is anyone
cheerful? Let him sing praise. ESV

Question 11

You often become part of the solution. You often realize and understand how
you could help.

Question 12: n/a

Question 13

Prayer is necessary. One could argue prayer first gets the attention of God and

then mobilizes His power on behalf of the unbeliever.
Question 14
Colossians 4:3 (1) give us opportunities, and (2) to proclaim the Gospel.
Eph 6:19-20 (1) give me the words, (2) declare gospel fearlessly
EXERCISE: n/a

LESSON 5 Why, What, Where, and When Should I Pray?
Question 1: n/a
LEADER: If you begin with a personal story, it should encourage others to share.
Question 2
In general we should pray about everything; we should not worry or fret, put pray. If it is impacting your life, then pray about it. But, remember if it is something trivial, then we must pray with the right motives. "Everything" in this context is meant to imply nothing is off limits.
Question 3
1. The coming of His kingdom
2. Daily bread
3   Forgiveness
4. Protection from temptation
Prayer in Matthew 6 vs. Jesus' prayer in John 17.
John 17 is *similar* to the Lord's Prayer (Mt 6)
- addressed to the Father
- in heaven
- hallowed be name
    divine will is paramount
- deliverance from evil
- power and glory belong to Father
- assumes God will hear prayer
- assumed contrast between kingdom and the world

Differences: no petition for forgiveness, help with temptation, or protection from the evil one.
Prayer requests in:
Ephesians 3:16-19
Ephesians 3:16-19 *that according to the riches of his glory he may grant you to be strengthened with*
power through his Spirit in your inner being, 17 so that Christ may dwell in your hearts through faith—that you, being rooted and grounded in love, 18 may have strength to comprehend with all the saints what is the breadth and length and height and depth, 19 and to know the love of Christ that surpasses knowledge, that you may be filled with all the fullness of God. ESV
Colossians 1:9-12
Colossians 1:9-12 *And so, from the day we heard, we have not ceased to pray for you, asking that you may be filled with the knowledge of his will in all spiritual wisdom and understanding, 10 so as to walk in a manner worthy of the Lord, fully pleasing to him, bearing fruit in every good work and increasing in the knowledge of God. 11 May you be strengthened with all power, according to his glorious might, for all endurance and patience with joy, 12 giving thanks to the Father, who has qualified you to share in the inheritance of the saints in light.* ESV

Question 4
So God knows our hearts, or rather so we know it. Sometimes we must verbalize something to understand better. I am clarifying my need/want for both myself and God.

Question 5
(1) We are afraid of being wrong, (2) we often don't know all the facts or details and are not sure how to pray, (3) not sure of God's will; (4) not want to put God on the spot!, and (5) it's easier.

Question 6
Mk 11:17 Pray in church; pray corporately with believers;
Mt 6:6   Pray privately, not showing off for others to see or hear
Lk 5:16   Pray privately, not showing off for others to see or hear
Mt 18: 19-20 Pray with others; there is special power in corporate prayer

Question 7
- We begin to "Love one another"
- We bear each others burdens (Gal 6:2)
- We build a committed relationship and sincere bond (Col 4:12-13)
- We encourage one another (Heb 10:24-25)
- We spiritually stimulate one another

Question 8
Since all believers are indwelt by the Holy Spirit, then God is certainly there among them.

Question 9
Since Jesus is already indwelling the believer, and that should be inherently understood, this may imply some additional or more intimate presence with those praying together.

Question 10
Pride (I can take care of myself; prayer is sign of weakness); Guilt; False humility (need or want is insignificant and not worthy of speaking to a holy almighty God about it.

Question 11
Believers come together to pray: in one accord, in agreement, unselfishly. They are all submitted and surrendered to the nature and will of God; in fellowship together under the umbrella of the administration of Christ.

Question 12

Genesis 18:22	standing
Mark 11:25	standing
Exodus 34:8	bowed to ground
Joshua 7:6	prostrate
Matthew 26:39	prostrate
1 Kings 8:54	kneeling
Luke 22:41	kneeling
2 Chronicles 6:12	standing before altar
1 Timothy 2:8	lifting up holy hands
Exodus 9:29	stretch out hands

Question 13
Very early in the morning.

Be bold and pray in the Spirit on all occasions.

Question 14

1. Beginning the day with prayer sets a positive tone and mindset for the rest of the day.

2. It implies prioritizing your spiritual growth and relationship with God before the demands and distractions of the day take over.

3. Morning prayer provides an opportunity to seek God's direction for the day, inviting His help in decision-making and the day's activities.

4. Praying in the morning allows you to ask for His Spirit to empower you in the face of the challenges and opportunities of the day.

5. Morning prayer helps you guard against distractions that may arise during in the day.

6. Jesus did it (e.g., Mark 1:35, Psalm 5:3).

7. Morning prayer prepares the heart for other spiritual disciplines during the day: worship, Bible study, evangelism, etc.

8. Beginning the day with prayer allows individuals to give the day to the Lord.

Question 15:

Obviously "without ceasing" or "continually" can't be literal because life wouldn't be able to happen or be sustained. In Daniel's day it was 3 times a day: *Three times a day he got down on his knees and prayed, giving thanks to his God, just as he had done before.* (Daniel 6:10) The Greek word here implies a meaning more like: uninterruptedly, without omission (on an appropriate occasion).

LESSON 6 What Results Can I Expect?

2 Kings 22:19

HOW ACT: (1) Penitent heart; (2) humbled yourself; (3) tore clothes; and 4) wept.

Psalms 10:17

HOW ACT: They were afflicted (suffering) and God inclined His ear.

Psalms 34:15, 17

HOW ACT: They were righteous.

Psalms 40:1

HOW ACT: They were patient.

Ps 65:1-2

HOW ACT: They gave praise to God; vows were completed.

1 Peter 3:12

HOW ACT: (1) righteous, and (2) not do evil

1 John 5:14-15

HOW ACT: We ask according to His will.

Hosea 5:3-7

I know Ephraim, and Israel is not hidden from me; for now, O Ephraim, you have played the whore; Israel is defiled. 4 Their deeds do not permit them to return to their God. For the spirit of whoredom is within them, and they know not the Lord. 5 The pride of Israel testifies to his face; Israel and Ephraim shall stumble in his guilt; Judah also shall stumble with them. 6 With their flocks and herds they shall go to seek the Lord, but they will not find him; he has withdrawn from them. 7 They have dealt faithlessly with the Lord; for they have borne alien children. Now the new moon shall devour them with their fields. ESV

Ans: (1) Defiled and corrupt; (2) Spirit of whoredom; (3) Not know the Lord; (4) Pride; (5) Sin in general result in guilt and stumbling; (6) Unfaithfulness.

Question 1 I believe it could have several implications or meanings. First, it very likely implies one must be a believer if you expect God to answer prayer. The only prayer God is likely to "hear" from a non-believer, is the sinner's prayer or a prayer of confession and repentance. Second, it could imply the difference between someone who sins occasionally for any number of reasons and the person involved in deliberate sin or ongoing rebellion. Then, there is the back-slidden believer who also might have a tough time being heard by a holy God.

Question 2 The issue here is not whether God really hears or listens. The point of the Scripture is that God is not going to do anything or answer the prayers or needs in question. Not hearing or listening is the writer's way of saying that "God won't consider your prayer."

Question 3

SIN. See Isa 59:2 and John 9:31 above

Psalms 66:17-18 *I cried to him with my mouth, and high praise was on my tongue. 18 If I had cherished iniquity in my heart, the Lord would not have listened.* ESV

Question 4a

Ps 118:5-6 (1) Set free from anguish and distress; (2) not to be afraid or fearful.

Psalms 138:3 I was strengthened (so I could be bold) and able to stand firm

Isa 58:9-11 (1) Guide you continually; (2) satisfy your needs and desires; (3) strengthen your physical frame; and (4) be like watered garden/spring of water . . . that does not fail

Dan 9:22-23 (1) Insight, (2) understanding

Question 4b

The context of Mt 6 is people who are hypocritical [(1)they pray loudly in Temple and (2) are seen at evening prayers]. The issue here is not to try to impress anyone else; the relationship is to be between you and God. The purpose and focus should be intimacy with the Father. "Reward you" or "repay you" seems to be another way to say that God will answer your prayer – this is not about additional rewards.

Question 5 Until Jesus' incarnation and ministry, the people did not really know about Jesus, the Christ, or His teaching statues, ordinances, etc. Therefore, this was all new. Jesus could not intercede for them until now. And, the Holy Spirit could not intercede for them until the people were indwelt. They did not know about Jesus and the indwelling Holy Spirit in the Old Testament.

Question 6 Don't be anxious about anything, e.g. health, general fears and worries, uncertainties, stress, persecution, mental or emotional anguish, and pressures of daily life . . . that brings peace and contentment

Question 7

2 Corinthians 4:16-18 FIX YOUR EYES ON JESUS! Put your trust in Him for all the past, present, and future challenges of life. Put it in God's hands!

Question 8

1 Peter 5:7 Give it all to God. Will our worrying about something solve the problem – No! He will provide because He cares.

Question 9

1. About your life
2. About what you will eat or drink
3. About your body – what you will wear

Why? Because life is more important than these things. God takes care of the birds, plants, flowers, grass, etc. He can certainly take care of us. He knows we need the necessities of life. Jesus suggests in 6:33ff that we seek first His kingdom and His righteousness and then all these things will be provided.

Question 10 n/a
DISCUSSION QUESTIONS
1. n/a
2. n/a
3. If God is the Creator, then He has created us for a reason and purpose. There is no logic in creating something and then allowing it to be destroyed.
4. Ps 86:5 To all who call upon the Lord.

1 Peter 4:19 Those who are doing good.

1 Cor 10:13 Normal temptation that all men must endure – not something special or unique.

LESSON #7 Praying With Boldness
DISCUSSION QUESTIONS
1.
He models the type of prayer God might answer.
Like the Lord's Prayer, we have a template or example of how to pray.
2.
He was respected.
He demonstrated honest or moral behavior.
He was fair or proper.
He was decent.
He was ethical, honest, or just.
He was noble, respected, or upstanding.
3.
Use answers to this prayer to do good (Eph 2:10).
Point people to Christ.
Glorify God.
Cause people to give thanks to God.
Serve others.
Develop Fruit of the Spirit.
4.
The Beatitudes of Mt 5:3-12 tell us what the Bible describes as a life worthy of blessing:

The Beatitudes
"Blessed are the poor in spirit, because the kingdom of heaven is theirs. 4 Blessed are those who mourn, because they will be comforted. 5 Blessed are the gentle, because they will inherit the earth. 6 Blessed are those who hunger and thirst for righteousness, because they will be filled. 7 Blessed are the merciful, because they will be shown mercy. 8 Blessed are the pure in heart, because they will see God. 9 Blessed are the peacemakers, because they will be called sons of God. 10 Blessed are those who are persecuted for righteousness, because the kingdom of heaven is theirs. 11 "Blessed are you

when they <u>insult you and persecute you</u> and falsely say every kind of evil against you <u>because of Me</u>. 12 Be glad and rejoice, because your reward is great in heaven. For that is how they persecuted the prophets who were before you. HCSB

5.

Use wealth properly. Pray for the strength and wisdom to use any expanded or additional wealth wisely, whatever the type or amount.

LEADER:

(1) What other areas of life (other than wealth or influence) could you ask to be expanded?

--Relationships.

--Ministry or service.

--Political success.

--Character (attributes).

--Job or career.

(2) In which one of these areas could you personally have the biggest impact? Why?

6.

Become more active in serving in church ministries.

Join a small group.

Learn how and be willing to share your faith story.

Reconcile with someone.

7. POSSIBLE AREAS:

Wealth, so it can be given away or used for ministry.

Character, such as mercy and empathy to serve others.

Ministry to serve and help others.

Relationships to encourage and build up one another.

Career to provide for needs.

Spiritual gifts to serve others at a high level.

Fruit of the Spirit to move you toward perfection.

Relationship with God so that we truly know Him.

Guard your lips so you cannot hurt others.

The Beatitudes.

8. n/a

9.

> **LEADER:** The following Scriptures speak against the excuse listed.
> SHY
>> 2 Tim 1:7 Pr 29:25; Jer 1:6-8; Heb 13:6.
>> 2 Tim 1:7 for God gave us a spirit not of fear [NIV says "timidity"] but of power and love and self-control. ESV
> NOT GIFTED
>> 1 Cor 1:26-29; 2 Cor 4:7, 12:6-7; Ro 12:5-8.
>> 1 Cor 1:27 *But God chose what is foolish in the world to shame the wise; God chose what is weak in the world to shame the strong.* ESV
> MIGHT FAIL
>> Mt 10:18-20; Ps 18:28-36; Nahum 1:7.
>> Matt 10:19 *When they deliver you over, do not be anxious how you are to speak or what you are to say, for what you are to say will be given to you in that hour.* ESV

Be bold and pray in the Spirit on all occasions.

TRUST or CONTROL
   Pr 3:5-6; Ps 27:1, 37:3-7, 56:3-4; Heb 11:1, 6; Ro 12:1.
   Pr 3:5 *Trust in the Lord with all your heart, and do not lean on your own understanding.*
TOO BUSY
   Mt 6:33-34; 11:28-30; Isa 40:29-31; Mk 10:27; Php 4:12-13;
   Heb 10:35-38
FEAR
   Mt 10:28; Heb 13:5-6

10.
Love of money or wealth.
Guarding my lips.
Guarding my eyes (immoral images are everywhere).
11. n/a
12.
(1) Asking for something that would require God to intervene in human history; (2) something that would require God's help for someone to achieve (e.g. courage, great wisdom;), that such person was not capable of doing on their own.
13.
For example would you pray:
That my life would bring praise and honor to God.
That I would know God.
That I have a right relationship with Christ.
That my worship is acceptable and heartfelt.
That I thirst for the truth of God's Word.
That I love God with all my heart, strength, mind, and soul.
That Christ is the central focus and reality of my life.
That I always have a thankful heart.

LESSON 8 How is Fasting Related to Prayer
Question 1
Jesus was preparing for his earthly ministry; He wanted to be at His spiritual peak when He *faced Satan*.
Question 2
(1) anoint head with oil, (2) wash face
Question 3
Yes. Mt 6:17 says "when" you fast, not "if" you fast. Lk 5:35 says they will fast, particularly after Jesus has ascended. Obviously while He was on earth they had direct access to Him – See Lk 5:34.
Question 4
13:3 – when they sent out workers into the world
14:23 – when they appointed elders
Question 5
(1) God is finally fedup with disobedience and sin (2) it is beyond the point of His mercy and compassion; (3) justice is demanded in love; and (4) it had no meaning to those fasting.
Jeremiah 14:10 *Thus says the Lord concerning this people: "They have loved to wander thus; they have not restrained their feet; therefore the Lord does*

not accept them; now he will remember their iniquity and punish their sins."
ESV
AGAIN: the problem is sin.

Question 6
Problems can develop if it is: 1) done regularly and habitually; (2) done very rigidly; or (3) done without thought, focus, or attention. The Result: the practice becomes devoid of any impact on heart or soul. Following a law or regulation was not the real purpose – heart change was the goal.

Question 7
(1) Trying to force God's hand; (2) trying to get their own way; (3) trying to leverage fasting to have intentional sin forgiven; and (4) substituting fasting for sinning.

Question 8
The sin was pride. He wanted to be seen, impress others, and exalt himself.

Question 9
The focus should <u>not</u> be on yourself, rather it should be on God.

Question 10
Isaiah 58:6-7 Philippians 2:3-4
Others, not yourself! NOTE: The problem is the same in both the Old and New Testaments in both questions above.

LESSON 9 What should be the purpose of our fast?
Ezra 8:23 To be heard by God.
Matt 4:1-2 To be protected from or strengthened for the coming temptation.
Joel 2:12 To return to and come closer to God.
Psalms 69:10 To be humbled. NOTE: here it specifically says that fasting produced humbling and that is also said in Ezra 8:21.
Ezra 8:21 To humble themselves.
Psalms 35:13 But I, when they were sick—I wore sackcloth; I afflicted myself with fasting; I prayed with head bowed on my chest. ESV
Luke 2:37 To seek enlightenment. They used worship, fasting, and prayer to seek the heart of God.
Zechariah 7:5 To honor, glorify, and exalt God.

Question 1
The purpose of the fasting was to elevate God's presence in the lives of His followers.

Question 2
    1. Bring justice (overcome bonds of wickedness).
    2. Remove or break the yoke (unfair burdens).
    3. Free the oppressed.
    4. Share food.
    5. Provide shelter for homeless.
    6. Clothe the naked.
    7. Provide for family (not hide from own flesh and blood).

Question 3
They could all apply. The importance or existence of any particular reason would be determined and influenced by geographic location and the local needs.

Question 4
Matthew 25:35-46 For I was hungry and you gave me food, I was thirsty and

you gave me drink, I was a stranger and you welcomed me, 36 I was naked and you clothed me, I was sick and you visited me, I was in prison and you came to me.' 37 Then the righteous will answer him, saying, 'Lord, when did we see you hungry and feed you, or thirsty and give you drink? 38 And when did we see you a stranger and welcome you, or naked and clothe you? 39 And when did we see you sick or in prison and visit you?' 40 And the King will answer them, 'Truly, I say to you, as you did it to one of the least of these my brothers, you did it to me.' 41 "Then he will say to those on his left, 'Depart from me, you cursed, into the eternal fire prepared for the devil and his angels. 42 For I was hungry and you gave me no food, I was thirsty and you gave me no drink, 43 I was a stranger and you did not welcome me, naked and you did not clothe me, sick and in prison and you did not visit me.' 44 Then they also will answer, saying, 'Lord, when did we see you hungry or thirsty or a stranger or naked or sick or in prison, and did not minister to you?' 45 Then he will answer them, saying, 'Truly, I say to you, as you did not do it to one of the least of these, you did not do it to me.' 46 And these will go away into eternal punishment, but the righteous into eternal life." ESV

Question 5:

Deuteronomy 9:18 Because of sin and doing evil.

1 Samuel 7:6 The personal and corporate sin of Israel.

Nehemiah 9:1-2 Their sin and the sin of the fathers.

Acts 13:2-3 Appointing individuals as missionaries and consecrating them unto God.

2 Chronicles 20:3-4 To seek help from God.

1 Corinthians 7:5 To devote yourself to prayer.

Daniel 9:3, 22-23   For insight and understanding (wisdom).

Question 6

Anything that requires drawing near to God! Anything that requires the power of God. Anytime a believer wants God to know they are serious about their prayer needs.

Question 7

Certainly, the issues and circumstances are just different. We need to fast and pray for the church, our country, government officials, church leaders, the lost, the poor . . .

LESSON 10   How to Solve Problems Through Prayer

Question 1

Mt 6:10 Daily bread.

Mt 6:12 Forgive debts (sin).

Mt 6:13 Protection from temptation and Satan.

Question 2

To seek the Lord. See 2 Chronicles 19:3 and 20:3-4

Question 3

(1) spend time in prayer

(2) in His Word (gain guidance, knowledge, understanding , and wisdom)

(3) in worship (praise and thanksgiving)

(4) in walking worthy with Him – living in obedience to His teachings

(5) in serving others (loving one another); being merciful

Question 4:

(1) Proclaim a fast in community (throughout all Judah).

(2) Come together to seek God; assembled the people "from all the cities."
(3) Addressed the people in the house of the Lord.

Question 5

God-centered; focus on God.

Question 6

Put on the full armor of God: Belt of <u>Truth</u>; Breastplate of <u>Righteousness</u>; <u>Gospel of Peace</u>; Shield of <u>Faith</u>; Helmet of <u>Salvation</u>; Sword of the Spirit (<u>God's Word</u>); <u>Pray in the Spirit</u>; <u>Keep alert</u>; <u>Persevere</u>.

<u>Ephesians 6:10-19</u> *Finally, be strong in the Lord and in the strength of his might. 11 Put on the whole armor of God, that you may be able to stand against the schemes of the devil. 12 For we do not wrestle against flesh and blood, but against the rulers, against the authorities, against the cosmic powers over this present darkness, against the spiritual forces of evil in the heavenly places. 13 Therefore take up the whole armor of God, that you may be able to withstand in the evil day, and having done all, to stand firm. 14 Stand therefore, having fastened on the belt of truth, and having put on the breastplate of righteousness, 15 and, as shoes for your feet, having put on the readiness given by the gospel of peace. 16 In all circumstances take up the shield of faith, with which you can extinguish all the flaming darts of the evil one; 17 and take the helmet of salvation, and the sword of the Spirit, which is the word of God, 18 praying at all times in the Spirit, with all prayer and supplication. To that end keep alert with all perseverance, making supplication for all the saints, 19 and also for me, that words may be given to me in opening my mouth boldly to proclaim the mystery of the gospel,* ESV

REMEMBER: our struggle is against the spiritual forces – not human!

Question 7

19:7 – "Let the fear of the Lord be upon you."
19:9 – "Thus you shall do it in the fear of the Lord, in faithfulness, and with your whole heart."

Question 8

The Lord Delivered Judah!

20:24 *When Judah came to the watchtower of the wilderness, they looked toward the horde, and behold, there were dead bodies lying on the ground; none had escaped.* ESV

CHALLENGE:

(1) Unbeliever: sin and unbelief.
(2) believer: (a) sin, (b) being right with God, (c) obedience.

Be bold and pray in the Spirit on all occasions.

Free PDF
MAKE WISE DECISIONS
[Get the ebook version for 99 cents]

Consequences Shape Lives.

This book discusses the nature of decisions and explores eight essential questions to make better decisions.

You are a few decisions away from transforming your life. You can make better decisions! This resource has sections on what makes a poor decision, questions to ask yourself, traps to avoid, short and sweet decisions, the wise decision framework, and twenty ways to be wise. It also has a handy decision-making checklist. (12 pages)

Free PDF: https://getwisdompublishing.com/resource-registration/

Kindle ebook for 99 cents: https://www.amazon.com/dp/B0FG8NC53J

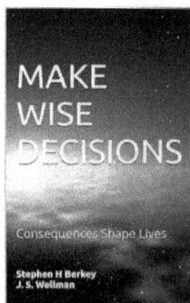

Ebook

Free PDF

Ten Steps to Wise Choices
Timeless Wisdom. Practical Tools. Lasting Impact.

Free PDF
Life Improvement Principles
[Get the ebook version for 99 cents]

You can live your best life!

Welcome to a journey of discovery! In case you have forgotten, your actions have consequences. Unlock your potential! This book (60+ pages) provides the overview of all our strategies and wisdom principles to live your best life. You *can* transform your life! Get your wisdom-based roadmap to a better life and unlock all the possibilities for growth and success.

Free PDF: https://getwisdompublishing.com/resource-registration/

Kindle ebook for 99 cents:
https://www.amazon.com/dp/B0FG883KZM

Ebook

Free PDF

Make it your life goal to be the best you can be!

Discover Wisdom and live the life you deserve.

Be bold and pray in the Spirit on all occasions.

What Next?

Continue Your Journey

Continue Study in the *Jesus Follower* Series
The Jesus Follower Bible Study Series
https://www.amazon.com/dp/B0DHP39P5J

Be Challenged by the *OBSCURE* Series
The *OBSCURE* Bible Study Series
https://www.amazon.com/dp/B08T7TL1B1

Tackle Wisdom-Driven Life Change
Apply Biblical Wisdom to Live Your Best Life!
"Effective Life Change"
https://www.amazon.com/dp/1952359732

Know What You Should Pray
Personal Daily Prayer Guide
https://www.amazon.com/What-Should-Pray-Personal-Journal/dp/1952359260/

Decide to be the Very Best You Can Be
The Life Planning Series
https://www.amazon.com/dp/B09TH9SYC4

You Can Help:
SOCIAL MEDIA: Mention The Jesus Follower Bible Study Series on your social platforms. Include the hashtag #jesusbiblestudy so we are aware of your post.

FRIENDS: Recommend this series to your family, friends, small group, Sunday School class leaders, or your church.

REVIEW: Please give us your honest review at
https://www.amazon.com/dp/1952359562

Be bold and pray in the Spirit on all occasions.

The OBSCURE Bible Study Series
Continue your journey through the hidden wisdom of Scripture with the OBSCURE Series.

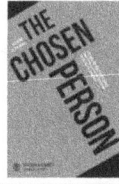

Blasphemy, Grace, Quarrels & Reconciliation: The lives of first-century disciples.
This book presents Joseph of Arimathea, Joanna, Ananias, Hymenaeus, and Cornelius (a centurion). It illustrates the nature and challenges of life as a first-century disciple.

The Beginning and the End: From creation to eternity.
This book has four lessons from Genesis and four from Revelation covering creation, rebellion, grace, worship, and eternity. God is leading us to worship in the Throne Room.

God at the Center: He is sovereign and I am not.
This book examines the virgin birth, worship, prayer, the sovereignty of God, compromise, and trust. God is at the center of all these stories. He is at the center of our lives.

Women of Courage: God did some serious business with these women.
This book examines the lives of Jael, Rizpah, the woman of Tekoa, Tabitha, Shiphrah, and Lydia. These women exhibit great courage and faithfulness. God used them in amazing ways.

The Beginning of Wisdom: Your personal character counts.
In this book we find courage, loyalty, thankfulness, love, forgiveness, and humility. Personal character counts. Decisions have consequences. Wisdom will help us stand firm in our faith.

Miracles & Rebellion: The good, the bad, and the indifferent.
God hates sin and loves to heal the faithful. The rebellion of Korah, Haman, and Alexander compare to the healing stories of Aeneas, a slave girl, and the crippled man at Lystra.

The Chosen People: There is a remnant.
This book concentrates mostly on Israel in the Old Testament, but also covers some interesting subjects as Lucifer, Michael the archangel, and Job's wife.

The Chosen Person: Keep your eyes on Jesus.
The focus is on Jesus and the superiority of Christ. We investigate Melchizedek, the disciples on the road to Emmaus, Nicodemus, and the criminal on the cross.

WEBSITE: http://getwisdompublishing.com/products/
AMAZON: www.amazon.com/author/stephenhberkey

Life Planning Series

Read these books if you want to live a better life.

The primary audience for this series is the secular self-help market, but the concepts are Christian based.

CHOOSE FAITH	**For the spiritual seeker and those with spiritual questions.** *Your Spiritual Guidebook For Questions About Religion, God, Heaven, Truth, Evil, and the Afterlife.* https://www.amazon.com/dp/1952359473
CHOOSE CORE VALUES	**Core values will drive your life.** https://www.amazon.com/dp/195235949X

Other Titles in the Life Planning Series

CHOOSE Integrity
CHOOSE Friends Wisely
CHOOSE The Right Words
CHOOSE Good Work Habits
CHOOSE Financial Responsibility
CHOOSE A Positive Self-Image
CHOOSE Leadership
CHOOSE Love and Family
LIFE PLANNING HANDBOOK A Life Plan Is The Key To Personal Growth https://www.amazon.com/gp/product/1952359325

Go to:

https://www.amazon.com/dp/B09TH9SYC4

to get your copy.

Be bold and pray in the Spirit on all occasions.

Personal Daily Prayer Guide
Prayer Resource and Journal

This is a great resource to kick-start your prayer life!

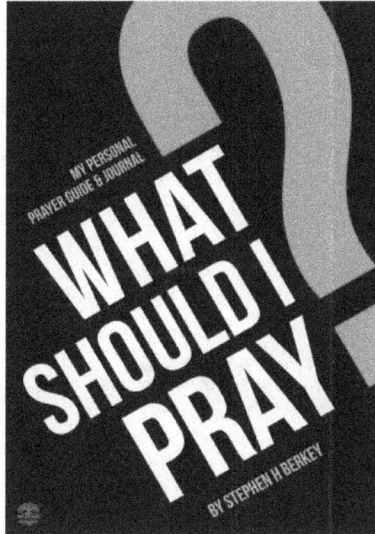

Know what to pray.
Pray based on Bible verses.
Strengthen your prayer life.
Access reference resources.
Pray with eternal implications.
Write your own prayers if desired.
Organize and focus your prayer time.
Learn what the Bible says about prayer.
Find encouragement and advice on how to pray.
Reduce frustration and distraction in your prayer time.

Get your copy today!

https://www.amazon.com/What-Should-Pray-Personal-Journal/dp/1952359260/

Be bold and pray in the Spirit on all occasions.

Acknowledgments

My wife has patiently persevered while I indulged my interest in writing. Thank you for all your help and assistance.

Our older daughter has been an invaluable resource. She has also graciously produced our website at www.getwisdompublishing.com

Our middle daughter designed the covers for most of my books, but I gave her a vacation on this Series. We are very grateful for her help, talent and creativity.

Notes

1 *E. M. Bounds

2 *Words of Wisdom – In the assignment lies the answer*; JAMAC 876, From movie: Evan Almighty.

3 *E. M. Bounds, p 31.

4 *E. M Bounds, p 48.

5 *E. M. Bounds, p19.

6 *E. M. Bounds.

7 Nelson's Bible Dictionary.

8 *E. M. Bounds, p 74.

9 SOURCE: Lord's Prayer Guideposts, Dr. David Jeremiah.

Purpose in Prayer, E. M. Bounds, Baker Book House, Grand Rapids MI, (New Edition), Copyright 1991 by Baker Book House Company, ISBN: 0-8010-1010-1. NOTE: For nearly 100 years E. M. Bounds' books on prayer have stimulated and inspired the church to pray. He was a man of God who lived to pray. Edward McKendree Bounds (1835-1913) began each day with three hours of prayer.

About the Author

Steve attended church as a child and accepted Christ when he was 10 years old. But his walk with Jesus left a lot to be desired for the next 44 years. In 1994 he "wrestled" with God for some period of months and in September of that year totally surrendered his life to Jesus.

In 1996 he was so driven to study God's Word that he attended the Indianapolis campus of Trinity Evangelical Divinity School (Chicago) to earn a Certificate of Biblical Studies. His hunger for God's Word led him to lead and write all his own Bible studies for his small group. He has been a Bible study leader for the past 25 years.

After 25 years as an actuary, and 20 years as an entrepreneur, he began his third career as an author in 2020, when he published The OBSCURE Bible Study Series. The Jesus Follower Bible Study Series was completed in early 2025. He is a member of The Church at Station Hill in Spring Hill, TN, a regional campus of Brentwood Baptist (Brentwood TN).

"Get Wisdom Publishing is dedicated to being the trusted source of wisdom-driven books that inspire growth, guide decisions, and empower readers to live with purpose and fulfillment."

Contact Us

Website: www.getwisdompublishing.com

Email: info@getwisdompublishing.com

Facebook: Get Wisdom Publishing

Author's Page:
www.amazon.com/author/stephenhberkey

Amazon's Jesus Follower Bible Study Series page:
https://www.amazon.com/dp/B0DHP39P5J

*"Go beyond devotionals.
Experience biblical wisdom in action!"*

GETWISDOM
PUBLISHING

www.ingramcontent.com/pod-product-compliance
Lightning Source LLC
Chambersburg PA
CBHW060322050426
42449CB00011B/2601